THE PLACE OF BONHOEFFER

Problems and Possibilities in His Thought

The

PROBLEMS AND

Place of Bonhoeffer

POSSIBILITIES IN HIS THOUGHT

Edited and Introduced by MARTIN E. MARTY

with: PETER BERGER

GEORGE FORELL

REGINALD FULLER

WALTER HARRELSON

FRANKLIN LITTELL

JAROSLAV PELIKAN

FRANKLIN SHERMAN

ASSOCIATION PRESS • • • NEW YORK

ACKNOWLEDGMENTS

This symposium of critical essays on the theological literature of Dietrich Bonhoeffer (1906-1945) was occasioned by a suggestion of William Hamilton of Colgate-Rochester Divinity School after the appearance of his *The New Essence of Christianity*. An interpreter of the prison letters of Bonhoeffer, Hamilton successfully points to the career-long continuities of Bonhoeffer's christological motifs—continuities which are part of the main theme of this book. I thank him for the suggestions and encouragement, in which he was joined by James Rietmulder who saw to the fruition of Hamilton's idea. I am also grateful to the seven authors who, responding from the several theological disciplines, prepared the critical essays and to the various publishers for permission to quote excerpts from the writings of Bonhoeffer and others.

WORKS OF BONHOEFFER

Gesammelte Schriften, I-IV, Eberhard Bethge, ed. (Munich: Chr. Kaiser Verlag, 1958-1961). These writings are not referred to except when a necessary point could not be illumined without such reference. This was done for but one reason: this book is conceived as, in part, an introduction to Bonhoeffer's thought for a general audience. In that case, widest interest must be presupposed for the easily accessible works listed below.

Sanctorum Communio: Eine dogmatische Untersuchung zur Soziologie der Kirche (Munich: Chr. Kaiser Verlag, 1954). A translation to appear, at least in England, is under way but was not ready for citation now by Professor Berger. (William Collins will be the British publisher.)

Act and Being, Bernard Noble, tr., Introduction by Ernst Wolf (New York: Harper & Brothers, 1962).

Creation and Fall, John C. Fletcher, tr. (New York: The Macmillan Company, 1959).

Cost of Discipleship, The, Reginald H. Fuller, tr. (New York: The Macmillan Company, 1948). Second edition, 1959.

Temptation, Kathleen Downham, tr. (New York: The Macmillan Company, 1955).

Life Together, John Doberstein, tr. (New York: Harper & Brothers, 1954).

Ethics, Neville Horton Smith, tr. (New York: The Macmillan Company, 1955).

Prisoner for God, Reginald H. Fuller, tr. (New York: The Macmillan Company, 1957).

Contents

Acknowledgments   5

Works of Bonhoeffer   6

1

Introduction   9
Problems and Possibilities in Bonhoeffer's Thought
     MARTIN E. MARTY

2

The Question: Who is Christ for Us Today?   25
Bonhoeffer's History, Church, and World
     FRANKLIN H. LITTELL

3

The Social Character of the Question Concerning
     Jesus Christ   51
Sociology and Ecclesiology
     PETER BERGER

4

The Methods of Asking the Question Concerning
     Jesus Christ   81
Act and Being
     FRANKLIN SHERMAN

5

The Source of Answers to the Question Concerning
    Jesus Christ   113
    Bonhoeffer and the Bible
    WALTER HARRELSON

6

The Early Answer to the Question Concerning Jesus
    Christ   143
    Bonhoeffer's Christologie of 1933
    JAROSLAV PELIKAN

7

The Christian in the Church Responding to the An-
    swer in Jesus Christ   167
    Liturgy and Devotion
    REGINALD H. FULLER

8

The Christian in the World Responding to the An-
    swer in Jesus Christ   197
    Realized Faith, the Ethics of Dietrich Bonhoeffer
    GEORGE W. FORELL

1

Introduction: Problems and Possibilities in Bonhoeffer's Thought

By Martin E. Marty

> The thing that keeps coming back to me is, what is Christianity, and indeed what is Christ, for us to-day?
> —Dietrich Bonhoeffer, 1944

> Dietrich Bonhoeffer, a Witness of Jesus Christ among his brothers. Born 4 February 1906 in Breslau; Died 9 April 1945 in Flossenbürg.
> —A plaque erected by his friends

> Bonhoeffer was a very sophisticated theologian, at home in all the niceties of theological speculation.
> —Reinhold Niebuhr, 1948

WHAT is the place of Dietrich Bonhoeffer? The question is no longer important for his place in the "Modern Acts of the Apostles." [1] There it is secure. It is not important in any sort of status scale of theologians: was he a major-minor theologian or a minor-major theologian? Or, even worse, must it be decided whether or not he was *the* theologian for our day, as overzealous admirers have suggested? By speaking of the place of Bonhoeffer the eight writers of this book are trying to locate his methods and emphases in the various disciplines of theological study. However important other questions may be,

9

these are the only ones that will preoccupy us in the present work.

If one wishes to make of any theologian the be-all and end-all of theological inquiry, it is precarious to embark on an evaluative effort. If one has the distance, the serenity, the willingness to see Bonhoeffer in the age-long sequence of witnesses to Jesus Christ in the theological disciplines less is hazarded but more is gained. If the first intention is the only one, then Bonhoeffer's students must constantly be looking over their shoulders to see how his current fortunes are running where matters of repute are discussed. If the second intention prevails, his students may do justice to his own brief, fragmentary, dramatic career; they may see what contribution he can make to Church and world in varying climates of opinion.

That Bonhoeffer deserves critical analysis as "a very sophisticated theologian" goes without saying. Perhaps only the European triumvirate of Karl Barth, Emil Brunner, and Rudolf Bultmann and the American triumvirate of Reinhold Niebuhr, Paul Tillich, and H. Richard Niebuhr have been more studied, invoked, and analyzed than Bonhoeffer in the past quarter-century. Younger European and American Christian thinkers often seem to be divided into two camps: those who acknowledge their debt to Bonhoeffer and those who are indebted but who obscure the traces to their source. Certainly in seminary halls, at student retreats, on college campuses, on the pages of ecumenical youth journals, in the fraternities of younger ministers few names must be conjured with so frequently as Bonhoeffer's.

If his name appeared at first as a hero or saint, in the second phase he is being taken seriously as he would wish to have been: as a professional theologian. On this level his thought must be subjected to analysis and criticism on the same plane as anyone else's. In the pages that follow, it may seem as if not all his thought stands up too well under such scrutiny. If so, it must also be remembered that men from six or seven theological disciplines are being called in to discuss one man who was reasonably at home with all of them. Is it possible for any one theologian to be a guide down all these paths?

It may be advantageous to the various types of readers who approach this book (from those gaining new acquaintance with Bonhoeffer's thought to those thoroughly at home with it) to locate the place of *The Place of Bonhoeffer*. It is not the first study. In Europe circles of his admirers prepared three collections of essays, *Die Mündige Welt*.[2] In the United States the best analysis to date can be found in the Chicago Theological Seminary *Register*, February, 1961. Bonhoeffer's friend, correspondent, and editor Eberhard Bethge delivered these Alden-Tuthill lectures; in general, authors in this volume would find Bethge's the most congenial interpretation. A longer but more modest evaluation is John Godsey's *The Theology of Dietrich Bonhoeffer*.[3] Godsey largely contents himself with skeining together Bonhoeffer's biography with condensations of the books. These condensations are less necessary now because almost all the books are easily available in English. When Godsey does come to evaluate he is not far from Bethge or the present authors in viewpoint.

In the present study, for the first time in the United States, a number of Christian thinkers were gathered to analyze Bonhoeffer's theological achievement for publication. All of them have a long familiarity with his work, are basically congenial toward it, but are not associated in the public eye with any "Bonhoeffer mystique"—an important element in the critical distance that was here sought. The general intentions of the volume were made clear to them; beyond that, they were free to develop their positions independently of each other and without editorial limitation. There are few contradictions in their final products; there are slight variations in degrees of enthusiasm for Bonhoeffer's achievements in their respective disciplines. Each contributor agreed to place Bonhoeffer in the history of theology and not to see him as the great theo-

logian of the age. We believe that laymen, students, seminarians, ministers—who will be reading Bonhoeffer anyhow, if
publishers' sales curves are any indication—will profit from the
methodological questions raised in each essay.

Now, to the place of Bonhoeffer. After reading these essays
I have come to the conclusion that he could well be nominated
"the theologian of the age of displacement." It is difficult to
locate his thought, because of its essential catholicity. Several
examples are of worth.

First, he is being read and interpreted on both sides of the
Iron Curtain. One of the most ambitious studies is Hanfried
Müller's *Von Der Kirche Zur Welt,*[4] a curious endeavor to
take "religionless" Bonhoeffer of the theologian's later letters
and make him sound like a Marxist! The pictorial display at
the Humboldt-Universität's One Hundred Fiftieth Anniver-
sary moved "from Schleiermacher through Harnack to Bonhoeffer." The Berlin newspaper *Neue Zeit,* December 3 and
12, 1957, contained full-orbed attempts to take Bonhoeffer's
late prison letters and use their view of history as a charter for
Marxist society. Meanwhile, because of his consistent opposition to any dilution of the gospel of Jesus Christ, his stand
against totalitarianism, his defense of freedom, he is much admired by Christian participants in a free society.

If he is read in both East and West, so, too he is studied in
both Catholic (Orthodox and Roman) and Protestant Christian circles. Within Protestantism he has been regarded by
some as a lineal descendant of the nineteenth century's liberal
tradition (he studied under von Harnack, R. Seeberg, and
Lietzmann; though he repudiated many of their viewpoints,
he identified himself with others and was undeniably indebted
to them). Others regard him as a sort of Lutheran Karl Barth,
a neo-orthodox "radical conservative." Though fundamental-
ists are somewhat uneasy with his approach to the Bible, they
admire the resultant exegesis, and the unflinching loyalty to
Jesus Christ; meanwhile the liberal interest in Christian ethics

is confirmed by his lifework. As the line between liberal and conservative is crossed, so is the line between clerical and lay. After his first two academic dissertations, most of his theological writing has the kind of lucidity that makes him understandable also among those not professionally trained in theology. He has been the guiding force behind many of the European lay academy movements of renewal and behind much American student concern.

The persistent tension within the Church between the academic theologians and the parochial activists is slackened in the face of the Bonhoeffer corpus. Obviously he is "a very sophisticated theologian"; his *Act and Being* and *Sanctorum Communio*, though they lack maturity, certainly hold their own as intellectual creations. Yet he moved from the university to ecumenical work, to the training of ministers for the Church in secret illegal seminaries, to divesting himself of clerical mannerisms in identification with prisoners of all nations near the end of his life. Meanwhile, parish ministers who have been drawn by *Life Together* or *The Cost of Discipleship* have been willing to follow Bonhoeffer into more complex areas, typically the *Ethics*.

In the chief interest in this book—the concreteness of revelation and Christology—he performed an even more remarkable feat: somehow he seems to bridge between historic Calvinist-Lutheran lines, lines which remain intact in much current ecumenical discussion. He was consistently Lutheran in his rejection of the Calvinist formula, *Finitum non capax infiniti*: the finite is not capable of bearing or revealing the infinite. Yet he stated the problem of revelation in such a way that it is difficult to see much difference (on this point, that is) from the later Karl Barth in the latter's essay *The Humanity of God*.[5] This ability to see to the safeguarding of God's transcendence while asserting that it is *this* world that God creates, in which He is Incarnate, Crucified, Resurrected—in other words, to reject angelism and all theologies of pure transcendence or revelatory illusion—may be his enduring contribution to theological thought in our own time.

Finally, more than any other theologian of our time, he seemed to adopt modes of expression and types of questions which made him attractive across confessional, traditional, and national lines. The writers in this volume did not need to be chosen according to denomination. Alec Vidler and Ronald Gregor Smith in England and Reginald Fuller in America have led the English religious tradition to take him seriously. On the Continent "a very sophisticated theologian" like Gerhard Ebeling and a very popular one like Helmut Thielicke could draw richly from this resource. In the younger churches and on the mission fields he is one of the few Continentals who has been widely admired. In America the Arminian-Reformed-Lutheran distinctions erode in the light of interest in Bonhoeffer.

Between East and West, Protestant and Catholic, Liberal and Conservative, clergyman and layman, theologian and activist, Calvinist and Lutheran, across the ecumenical spectrum he has stood as a symbol. Has he had no separate theological identity? Does he merely serve the needs of those who would re-create him in the light of their own interests? Not at all. He is appealing to all these among other reasons because he empathized with the newer kind of Christian believer and thinker, the dislocated, displaced inhabitant of a secular world.

His yearning for "place" is apparent in one of the strange classical references to which he returned again and again. Almost at the beginning of his work, in an outline from Barcelona in 1929 [6] he refers to the giant Antäus; nearly at the end Antäus reappears in a fragment of a drama written at the Tegel prison in 1943. Antäus of Libya, the son of Poseidon, forced passing strangers to wrestle with him. When thrown, he would draw fresh strength from contact with Mother Earth, and thus proved invincible. (Heracles learned the source, lifted him, and crushed him to death.) To Bonhoeffer, Antäus represented earthiness, concreteness, sanity, place, "ground under the feet" in the Christian theological and ethical quest.

Many people, many Christians have empathized with Bonhoeffer in this yearning for ground beneath the feet; social and psychic forces in our time tend to deny it, but even the quest remains important. At the beginning of the collection of letters and papers from prison Bethge has placed Bonhoeffer's summary "After ten years."

> Surely there has never been a generation in the course of human history with so little ground under its feet as our own. Every conceivable alternative seems equally intolerable. We try to escape from the present by looking entirely to the past or the future for our inspiration, and yet, without indulging in fanciful dreams, we are able to wait for the success of our cause in quietness and confidence. It may be however that the responsible, thinking people of earlier generations who stood at a turning-point of history felt just as we do, for the very reason that something new was being born which was not discernible in the alternatives of the present.[7]

In a world of displacement Bonhoeffer rejected angelism, pure transcendence, revelatory illusion from the first. October, 1931: "This invisibility smashes us indeed. . . . This madness of being thrown back again and again on the invisible God himself—who can stand that anymore?" [8] It led him to pursue the concrete nature of revelation and to focus on Christology: "Indeed, what is Christ for us today?"

Bonhoeffer's rejection of any sort of cosmic nostalgia, of most romantic yearnings for the past (there are a few exceptions in the letters), of false dreams for the future; his willingness to accept what God gave in the present has caused others in a generation without ground beneath its feet to identify with him. It has also led him and his students to pursue an analysis of history which has gathered many followers, drawn much attention, and in the eyes of some become the totality of what he represents. I refer to the understanding of a "world come of age," the maturation of secularity revealed in the last letters in *Prisoner for God*. Bonhoeffer, it is well known, foresaw the end of the religious phase in Western man's development and wanted to provide a theological base for the Christian displaced both spatially "from the ground of Western Civilization" and temporally from Christendom's unfolding.

As a prophet of nonreligious interpretation of biblical categories and Christian experience he has occasioned superficial dismissal by his critics and breathless, awe-full praise from many admirers. In the light of these letters which Karl Barth called "a particular thorn" some have dismissed him from the Christian fold entirely. Others—particularly in the exposed life of a coming American generation—have gone to the other extreme. They reject the whole Bonhoeffer corpus to this point and try to build a "worldly" ethic and secular systematic theology out of several enigmatic, fragmentary, intuitive projections in personal correspondence. In such an interpretation it is necessary to say that what is new in the late letters is utterly new; that it bears no continuities with the past. This seems to be psychologically untenable: does "a very sophisticated theologian" suddenly move out of his mentally furnished apartment; can he, as it were, "jump out of his skin"? Can he leave behind the multitude of hooks to which he has tagged his consciousness, his attitudes, his opinions? Is it fair to Bonhoeffer, the displaced theologian, to take away also the theological "ground beneath the feet" which remained in his devotion to a concrete revelation of a suffering and glorious God in Jesus Christ—in the middle of the world come of age?

The seven essayists whose works follow would say "no." None of them would minimize the dramatic and fruitful character of his late reflections. Bonhoeffer throughout his life tended to speak somewhat disparagingly of his earlier work. *Act and Being* he left behind within two or three years, even though continuities between it and the last letters are apparent. And in the last letters, although he spoke critically of some aspects of his work of a decade earlier before the formal "nonreligious" category appeared, he still would write, "Nevertheless, I stand by what I wrote." In short, though some would hold an interest in Bonhoeffer's nonreligious Christian quest *in spite of* his view of concrete revelation and humiliation-Christology, the writers of this book hold an interest in his nonreligious quest *because* of his view of a concrete revelation in Jesus Christ. This continuity provides the "ground beneath the feet" for Christian theology and ethics in the age of displacement, dislocation, uprootedness. Little energy is spent in the following pages on any polemic in defense of this viewpoint. It is implied throughout, however, in the interests of focusing on the enduring theme and thus actually enhancing the last creative directions Bonhoeffer took in his nonreligious phase. Because of his Christology Bonhoeffer was somehow "nonreligious" from the first—even in his writings on discipline and devotion!

By *religion* Bonhoeffer meant hyperindividualism, self-contained inwardness, bad conscience or the sin-sick soul as psychological *a prioris* for Christian experience, devotion to a particular metaphysic, stance, or piety. These belong to Christian advocacies of angelism, spirituality, pure transcendence in mysticism or Docetic theology. They never could belong to one who began by locating the theological question in the sociological setting of the Church! Yes, the later letters have newness but not unanticipated, breach-making newness. That is why they are doubly valuable to the people who stand in Eastern or Western, Catholic or Protestant, Lutheran or Calvinist, clerical or lay lineages!

Such an analysis of Bonhoeffer's thought rescues him from the kind of misfortunes to which his memory is being subjected and will be subjected in Europe. If he represents something utterly new and unique, not located in theological disciplines or related to historic concerns, he must be regarded either as demigod or obsolete idol. This has happened in a number of cycles already in Europe, and has caused many of the sane Christian thinkers there to regard him less seriously than they might both because of the antics of admirers and because there is not enough of resolution in the late letters to bear enduring scrutiny.

Such an analysis of Bonhoeffer's thought rescues him from a different kind of potential dismissal in America. Here there is less voguish interest in theologians; it is less necessary for one generation to demolish its predecessors or teachers than is the case in Europe. But if Bonhoeffer is exclusively associated with nonreligious interpretations of Christianity in a secular world it is possible that he be superficially dismissed in those times in America when—despite his apparent relevance— American secularity is shrouded in and masked by what looks like religion. In the 1950's America did not look as if it had "come of age," had moved beyond the religious question. Statesmen, scientists, entertainers seemd to need "God" as the "x" in their equations, as the lubrication for their processes. In such religious phases would Bonhoeffer have nothing to say? Yet it was precisely then that he was most eagerly listened to because of his Christology; his accent on the concrete revelation of a transcendent God in a suffering Savior, the man put forth for the world, spoke to our situation.

For American religiousness in the 1950's was what Gerhard Szczesny would call a subjective religiosity against which Bonhoeffer railed.

> A clear distinction can be made between objective and subjective kinds of religiosity. Those substitute religions which exhibit a fascination for the lawfulness of phenomena environmentally surrounding and conditioning man neglect to account for the interior life of the human person. On the other hand, substitute religions created by observers of interior psychological events tend to ignore

the material, biological and sociological relationships in which man is embedded. And both types, each according to the limitations of its perspective, ignore the question of man's position in the cosmos. From either of these pseudo-religious points of view this man-versus-cosmos issue has no significance. The objective systems reduce life's meaning to man's participation in scientific or quasi-scientific processes, whereas subjective ideologies see life's meaning in the unfolding of individual man's ability to experience and enjoy. The objective systems close their eyes to the individual's private fate and the subjective ones to the external factors of existence by which he is inescapably conditioned. Both skirt the problems which man must unremittingly try to solve in order to understand his existence within the cosmic frame.[9]

Bonhoeffer's Christology is an answer to Szczesny's misinterpretation (from the Christian viewpoint) of objective religiosity. But Szczesny's description is à propos the American religious revival's subjectivist cultism. "He's so sincere" became the inclusive religious category; man in the act of being religious was apotheosized. A generalized religion, religion-by-consensus, a cluster of sacred notions prevailed. Their net result was a glossing over of the essential secularity of American life. British author Eugene Rolfe spoke to this "world come of age" attitude: "Almost all of us nowadays conduct our lives for all practical purposes as if God did not exist." [10] It is at precisely this point that Bonhoeffer's christological interpretation brings to reveal what he meant by "nonreligiousness." He did not mean an uncritical baptism of the unredeemed world!

Since this is an American study, it may be necessary to set these concerns into the American context. If the American religious revival of the 1950's tended to drag God down to the level of man's projections ("Man Upstairs," "Living Doll," and other similarly near-blasphemous or blasphemous intimacies), is it not precisely the wrong therapy to assert of Bonhoeffer's "humiliation-Christology," his witness to God at the center of life? It would seem so, especially since—as it seems to me—one of the deficiencies of Bonhoeffer's last concerns is his inability to bring the fullness of Trinitarian witness to bear at all times on all points. Thus one of the classical Christian safeguards for transcendence seemed to be limited.

Yet, American religion in the past half-century has needed just Bonhoeffer's type of christological emphasis. Whether in our "religious" revival we carry the idea of God's transcendence almost to the point of his nonexistence ("Oh, my religion is much too deep inside me, much too spiritual . . . to have a part in my business, my politics, the world") or if we carry the idea of immanence to the point of identity, we are in similar situations. Gabriel Vahanian has pointed to the similarities. If God is dead (or so remote that he may as well be), then all is grace, everything is permissible. If God is only grace ("cheap grace" is Bonhoeffer's word for a doctrine carried to the point of identity!), again, everything is permissible. It must be remembered that Bonhoeffer's christological concern is born in a sociological one and moves to an ethical one. Religion asks, "How can I find a gracious God?" Christians in a world come of age ask, "Lord, what wouldst thou have me to do?"

His witness against Docetism, then, for all its risks (see the essay by Jaroslav Pelikan) is vital in the climate of American religiousness or spirituality glossing over secularity. In this light the two pervasive heresies of the last half-century here, Fundamentalism and Modernism, can be seen to share identities. Fundamentalism was Docetic in that in its view of Scripture and the humanity of Christ it did not really "let God be man." Modernism, similarly, in its reverence for "The Master," a gentle poet of the mystic Galilean hills, tended also—even if dogmatically it avoided reference to the "deity" of Christ—practically and devotionally to refuse really to "let God be man" in his concrete revelation in Jesus Christ, "The Man for Others" (Act and Being).

These are not problems only in America, though this is where they must be faced, where the masks are on over the face of secularity. Bonhoeffer in his second book showed his familiarity with the thought of Erich Przywara, S.J. His lifework can be seen to be a wrestling with Przywara's strictures against a Protestant contradiction. "Distinctive Lutheranism is dominated by the contradiction of a 'transcendent immanence' [*Finitum capax infiniti*], distinctive Calvinism by that of an 'immanent transcendence,' both, that is to say, by the wresting of the mystery enclosed in God alone to 'comprehensibilities' expressed in assurance of salvation." [11] From Przywara's viewpoint, Lutheran thought led to an identification of God with the historical process; Calvinism led to an uncompromising transcendence. Lutheran thought then would culminate in Hegel's "absorption of God" into atheism (the Marxist interpretation of Bonhoeffer?). Calvinist thought would culminate in man's encounter in solitude with "the unknown" (as in the misinterpretations of nonreligiousness?).

It would be unfortunate if a theological overeagerness to dramatize an aspect of Bonhoeffer's thought would destroy the witness he spent a lifetime developing. Thus in his third last letter, August 21, 1944, Bonhoeffer is meditating on two verses of Scripture, verses which many of his students and critics may have failed to regard because he only cites them. Numbers 11:23, "And the Lord said to Moses, 'Is the Lord's hand shortened? Now you shall see whether my word will come true for you or not.'" And II Corinthians 1:20: "For all the promises of God find their Yes in him. That is why we utter the Amen through him, to the glory of God." Bonhoeffer points to the key "in him," but behind it stands the "of God" and "to the glory of God."

> The God of Jesus Christ has nothing to do with all that we, in our human way, think he can and ought to do. We must persevere in quiet meditation on the life, sayings,

deeds, sufferings and death of Jesus in order to learn
what God promises and what he fulfils.[12]

This belongs to his "nonreligious" period. It differs hardly at
all from the concerns in the earliest formal writings—except
for the scope, which has moved from Christ for the Church to
Christ for the world! But the revelatory question remains the
same. In *Sanctorum Communio* God is *unverdinglichte*—not
at man's disposal in his majesty. Yet he existed in Christ personally *pro nobis*, for man.

Never did he put this distinction in better fashion than he
had already done in *Act and Being*. In it he gave the answer
to Przywara's metaphysical and formalistic concern for grace
and the clue toward which Calvinist and Lutheran (in this
picture ideal types for the Protestant options) could gravitate.
He did this by reference to the freedom of God which, without contradiction, remains "not at our disposal" and yet acts
toward man in the concrete revelation in Jesus Christ.

> The whole situation impels one to ask whether a formal-
> istic understanding of God's freedom in contingent reve-
> lation, conceived wholly in terms of the act, is really the
> proper groundwork for theology. In revelation it is a ques-
> tion less of God's freedom on the far side from us, i.e.
> his eternal isolation and aseity [being from itself], than of
> his forth-proceeding, his *given* Word, his bond in which
> he has bound himself, of his freedom as it is most strongly
> attested in his having freely bound himself to historical
> man, having placed himself at man's disposal. God is not
> free *of* man but *for* man. Christ is the Word of his free-
> dom. God *is there*, which is to say: not in eternal non-
> objectivity but (looking ahead for the moment) "have-
> able," graspable in his Word within the Church. Here a
> substantial comes to supplant the formal understanding
> of God's freedom.[13]

Przywara's concern was formal; Bonhoeffer's, substantial. In it
he pointed the way to a christological emphasis that is en-

hanced by an understanding of a "world come of age." Here
is where studies of Bonhoeffer seem to be locating themselves
most recently. Here is where the theologian of displacement
finds his place; in a time when there was no "ground beneath
the feet," this "deprovincialized Christ" [14] gave Bonhoeffer
the Antäus-like strength he longed for in a time which would
have denied him—but, in the end, could not.

The question, "Indeed what *is* Christ, for us today?" remains. These Bonhoeffer studies, it is hoped, will help American readers ask it—and answer it. Bonhoeffer's "end" question
comes at the beginning. It preoccupied his thoughts to the
last, until—as his executioners came for him at Flossenbürg—
he could say, "This is the end—for me the beginning of Life."

Notes for Essay 1

1 Quoted from Reinhold Niebuhr in John Godsey, *The Theology of Dietrich Bonhoeffer* (Philadelphia: The Westminster Press, 1960), p. 203.

2 Munich: Chr. Kaiser Verlag, 1956.

3 Philadelphia: The Westminster Press, 1960.

4 Leipzig: Verlag Keeler und Amelang, 1961.

5 Richmond, Va.: John Knox Press, 1960.

6 Dietrich Bonhoeffer, *Gesammelte Schriften*, Eberhard Bethge, ed. (Munich: Chr. Kaiser Verlag, 1958-1961), III (1960), 57.

7 Reprinted with the permission of the publisher, from *Prisoner for God: Letters and Papers from Prison*, pp. 13-14, by Dietrich Bonhoeffer, tr. by Reginald Fuller. Copyright 1953 by The Macmillan Company.

8 Bethge's translation, *Gesammelte Schriften* (*op. cit.*), I (1958), 61.

9 Gerhard Szczesny, *The Future of Unbelief* (New York: George Braziller, Inc., 1961), p. 93. Used by permission.

10 *The Intelligent Agnostic's Introduction to Christianity* (London: Hutchinson & Co., Ltd., 1959), p. 19.

11 See Przywara's essays *Ringen der Gegenwart* (Augsburg, 1929), II, 543-578 and "Das Katholische Kirchen Prinzip" in *Zwischen den Zeiten*, July, 1929, 277-302.

12 *Prisoner for God* (*op. cit.*), p. 183.

13 Dietrich Bonhoeffer, *Act and Being*, Bernard Noble, tr. (New York: Harper & Brothers, 1962), pp. 90-91.

14 Eckhard Minthe's phrase in reference to *Ethics*, p. 61.

2

The Question: Who *Is* Christ for Us Today?

Any interpretation, any study of Bonhoeffer which does not take seriously his definition of his concern will certainly do him an injustice. He makes that question unmistakably clear. His polemic against religiousness or religiosity was as enduring as this positive concern, but was ancillary to it. In that remarkable turning of the page (from 121 to 122 in the American version of *Prisoner for God*) where he poses the issue that has attracted so many to him he states it:

> You would be surprised and perhaps disturbed if you knew how my ideas on theology are taking shape. . . . The thing that keeps coming back to me is, what is Christianity, and indeed who is Christ, for us to-day? (Was mich unablässig bewegt, ist die Frage, was das Christentum oder auch wer Christus heute für uns eigentlich ist.)

In *Sanctorum Communio*, his first book, we shall see Bonhoeffer locating the question in the Church (instead of in the world as he was to do at the end). In *Act and Being*, his second, he was to locate the method of asking it in the light of theologies of action and essence. In his career-long biblical exposition (*The Cost of Discipleship*, and other writings) he was to find that the whole Scripture pressed Christ forward to him as the concrete embodiment of the answer. In his decisive lectures on Christology this is made clear in systematic lineaments, however much they would be reappraised in the last, "worldly" interpretation. In his liturgical and devotional works (such as *Life Together*) he would see the gathered, disciplined, retreating, inhaling, nurturing Church gaining strength to carry the question and answer out into the unprotected world. Finally, in *Ethics* he was to give the most concrete answers. In that chronological sequence we find the plot of this book and of the career of his question. We ask the last question first, to keep it constantly before us. To place the letters at the end *involves us in the danger of distorting the question, exaggerating the discontinuity between the time when it was asked in the Church to the time when it was asked in the world.*

Franklin Littell, formerly of Southern Methodist University and recently of Chicago Theological Seminary, has been asked to set these late prison letters into context. Dr. Littell, more than any other American, has stayed in close contact with the Europeans who resisted totalitarianism in the 1930's and 1940's. Bonhoeffer, the giant among the resistants, is thus "an old familiar friend" to Littell, who knew him at the time of his first American stay in 1931. Littell is therefore less inclined to approach late and early Bonhoeffers with the sense of radical distinction which someone who comes late to the late Bonhoeffer would do. As an advocate of the disciplined "free" Church that asks no prerogatives, privileges, or quarter from a secular world molded in a religious stamp, Littell himself comes close to working out a "worldly" interpretation for the United States as he has done in his most recent book From State Church to Pluralism.

By approaching the letters at the beginning instead of the end it becomes possible to see that although Bonhoeffer's interpretation of secularity may be new in the Christian world (at least in conjunction with such a "high" Christology!), his christological interpretation is the "nonreligious interpretation of the biblical terms," as Gerhard Ebeling has pointed out. It makes room for the "proper distinction between Law (religion) and Gospel (Jesus Christ), again as Ebeling has noted. It means that Bethge is correct in seeing his fundamental metaphor, "concretion of the revelation" elaborated against but one more—radically new—background.

All these have little to do with the Marxist interpretations of Bonhoeffer (Hanfried Müller and other East Zone Germans); the secularist interpretations (in many American student groups); the humanist interpretation (for which Bonhoeffer was scolded by, among others, Erich Müller-Gangloff and—in a way—Karl Barth).

By seeing the continuities in place of the discontinuities in Bonhoeffer's thought the contributors to this volume try to give the readers a place to stand to view the world and his world: and thus to prepare them for the real newness his last daring, tentative, fragmentary, intuitive, exciting prison thoughts implied for us!

So we begin with the last, which is also the first . . .

Bonhoeffer's History, Church, and World

By Franklin H. Littell

DURING the first half of the twentieth century, Christendom suffered more severe losses than at any other time for at least a millennium. The only period in church history comparable to recent decades would be the eighth and ninth centuries, when powerful Moslem peoples laid conquest fully half of Christendom before they were stopped at the gates of Europe. In the Mediterranean basin almost all the ancient centers of the Christian faith—Alexandria, Jerusalem, Antioch, Ephesus, and finally Constantinople—fell to Islam. In the early twentieth century, the totalitarian ideologies of Communism and Nazism (with variants such as Fascism) laid conquest whole peoples. Rome, Wittenberg, and Moscow ("the third Rome" of Orthodoxy) fell conquest. For a believing man, seeking to understand the purposes of God, several basic questions were posed by these developments:

- What was the *message* of such a fearful judgment?
- What might the appropriate response of Christian men be to the new situation?
- Wherein was the apostasy of the church that such a thing could happen to "Christian" nations?

27

• What new forms must be developed to make the gospel relevant, again, and this time in the world after Christendom disintegrated?

Dietrich Bonhoeffer's ministry was lived out in the midst of the early years of the Christian encounter with totalitarianism; and the full implications for preaching, for a Christian style of life, for the interpretation of history, are by no means clear nearly two decades after his death. His problem was complicated by the maturity of his devotion to responsible action. From the beginning he was stubbornly opposed to mere abstraction, to Christian principles, ideals, or proclamations separated from a community of witness, divorced from the concrete realities of the historical situation. He considered "religion"—a "spirituality" or "teaching" without a body—an enemy of true Christianity. As a Swiss scholar has put it, Bonhoeffer's message "consisted of the communication of the Word of God in a concrete way. That is why he was never content merely to evoke faith. No: faith is sometimes in danger of being taken to be abstract truth!" [1] At one time, Bonhoeffer's concerns seemed to point toward a new kind of monastic discipline. Later, his understanding of the incarnation led him to evaluate the natural forces and expressions of life more positively. What was consistent was his turn away from the idealistic and ideational to concrete realities.

It is frequently said that during the years which followed the collapse of the nineteenth-century continuum of Christ and culture, Christian thinkers rediscovered first the Bible, then the church, and then the laity. If the publication of Karl Barth's *Epistle to the Romans* (1919, 1923) symbolized the first stage of that process, Dietrich Bonhoeffer's *Life Together* (1938) may be said to be the mark of the second stage. The "rediscovery of the laity" came with the emergence of the Evangelical Academies and *Kirchentag* after his death, movements led in good part by men who had known and loved him in the German Student Christian Movement (DCSV) and in the Confessing Church (BK).

In his doctoral thesis, Sanctorum Communio, Bonhoeffer had already raised the problem of the church which he pursued further in Life Together. With his lifetime "turning away from the phraseological to the real," [2] he early suggested that "it would be good to begin a dogmatic treatise for once not with the doctrine of God but with the doctrine of the church, in order to make clear the inner logic of dogmatic construction." [3] He put the same issue again and again:

> God does not intend the history of single persons, but the history of the community of persons.[4]
> The Church is the new will of God for human beings.[5]
> Not religion, but revelation; not religious community, but church.[6]
> Since the ascension, Christ's place on earth has been taken by His Body, the Church.[7]

In Life Together the incarnational theology is pressed further. Christian brotherhood is "not an ideal, but a divine reality. . . . God hates visionary dreaming; it makes the dreamer proud and pretentious." [8] The only real authentication of spiritual fellowship is in the material. There is a view which sees

> . . . a danger of confusing and mixing the two spheres, whereas there can be no such danger in a purely spiritual fellowship. This idea, however, is a great delusion. According to all experience the truth is just the opposite. . . . A purely spiritual relationship is not only dangerous but also an altogether abnormal thing.[9]

Bonhoeffer was acutely aware of the theological challenge of Nazism as a gnostic philosophy,[10] with a strong emphasis upon "spirituality"—but a spirituality devoid of confessional integrity and connection with any historical communion. Article 24 of the NSDAP Party platform specifically espoused a nonsectarian religion to be distinguished carefully from any specific creeds or confessions (that is, from history). His earliest writings return frequently to the necessity of a witnessing community, of church discipline, of a binding brotherhood. This community is eschatological in atmosphere and in style. Church History thus derives its meaning not primarily from the past, not even from the present task, but from the last things.

> The Church of the Holy Scripture—and there is no other "Church"—lives from the end. Therefore it reads all Holy Scripture as the book of the end, of the new, of Christ. . . . The Bible is nothing but the book upon which the Church stands. This is its essential nature. . . .[11]

But the problematic which led him near the end to turn in prison to the blessedness of the created order, redeemed in Christ, was already there. He could not, when he pressed the issue, locate and limit the Word to a visible and clearly defined body of people—in the past, in the present, or even in the future.

> There comes a time for a church in which she may no longer be Volkskirche, and this time comes when the church in her volkskirchlich way can no longer see the way to press through to the voluntary church.[12]

To the determined champion of the gathered church, Bonhoeffer's final chapter in Sanctorum Communio is as disappointing as his intransigent opposition to the Nazi government's ecclesiastical policies was to the stubborn defenders of the traditional reading of Romans 13. The truth is that he was already exploring ways of thinking which would at the end lead him away from both asceticism and traditional sacramentalism.

> Life together under the Word will remain sound and healthy only where it does not form itself into a movement, an order, a society, a collegium pietatis, but rather

where it understands itself as being a part of the one, holy, catholic, Christian Church, where it shares actively and passively in the sufferings and struggles and promises of the whole Church.[13]

Quite evidently, then, Bonhoeffer was dissatisfied from the beginning with traditional formulations of the role of the church in the world and in history. Against the spiritualizing thrust of Nazism he stressed central Christian concerns, not being ashamed to use classical expressions and emphases to refute error. This came out most plainly, perhaps, in *The Cost of Discipleship*. Against the easy promiscuity of culture-religion he developed a restraint toward the world which was almost monkish, Franciscan:

> Having reached the end of the beatitudes, we naturally ask if there is any place on this earth for the community which they describe. Clearly, there is one place, and only one, and that is where the poorest, meekest, and most sorely tried of all men is to be found—on the cross at Golgotha. . . .
>
> The flesh resists this daily humiliation, first by a frontal attack, and later by hiding itself under the words of the spirit (i.e., in the name of "evangelical liberty"). We claim liberty from all legal compulsion, from self-martyrdom and mortification, and play this off against the proper evangelical use of discipline and asceticism; we thus excuse our self-indulgence and irregularity in prayer, in meditation and in our bodily life. But the contrast between our behaviour and the word of Jesus is all too painfully evident. We forget that discipleship means estrangement from the world, and we forget the real joy and freedom which are the outcome of a devout rule of life.[14]

In one of his last letters (written July 21, 1944) he was to refer to that accent somewhat critically:

> I thought I could acquire faith by trying to live a holy life, or something like it. It was in this phase that I wrote

The Cost of Discipleship. Today I can see the dangers
of this book, though I am prepared to stand by what I
wrote.[15]

Yet even at the last he was sustained by a lifetime of daily
study and devotional discipline. He was constantly aware of
the Church Year. His letters referred frequently to the *Losung*
of the day; the Psalms and hymns were used regularly; daily
devotions were maintained.

There can be no doubt that the daily Bible passages published by the Moravian Brethren, for example, are a real
blessing to all who have ever used them. This was discovered by many to their grateful astonishment particularly
during the church struggle.[16]

He referred to his schedule of arising at 6:00 A.M., doing the
"daily dozen," taking a cold washdown, not yielding to the
temptation to become disoriented, disordered.[17] As with Luther, the early monastic accent remained a mark of personality
much more than he himself probably realized. On the other
hand, from the start he knew that it was not enough and that
the true accent of the Word was elsewhere. That true accent
is summed up in the pregnant statement that Christ did not
die for the church, but for the world.

Dr. George Bell, Bishop of Chichester and the friend to
whom he communicated the conspirators' plans to overthrow
Hitler, later put Bonhoeffer's basic concern in this way:

For Bonhoeffer . . . the church as a living force in this
world entirely depends on her *this-sidedness.* Of course,
Bonhoeffer understood this term neither in the sense of
modern liberal theology nor in the sense of the National
Socialist creed. Both modern liberal theology and secular
totalitarianism hold pretty much in common that the
message of the Bible has to be adapted, more or less, to
the requirements of a secular world.[18]

Heinz Zahrnt, in writing a tribute ten years after Bonhoeffer's death in Flossenbürg, put it this way: "There have been martyrs who called the world to the church. Dietrich Bonhoeffer is a martyr who called the church to the world." [19] Bonhoeffer's own turning from a deliberate asceticism to a consuming concern for a world come of age was clearly indicated in his own words in the *Nachfolge*:

> Cheap grace is the deadly enemy of our church. Today we are fighting for the grace that is precious.
> Cheap grace is preaching forgiveness without penitence, baptism without church discipline, communion without confession of sin, absolution without personal confession.
> Cheap grace is grace without discipleship, grace without the cross, grace without the living incarnated Jesus Christ.
> With the expansion of Christianity and the growing worldliness of the church the consciousness of a precious grace was gradually lost. The world was Christianized; grace became the common property of a Christian world —cheap to have.
> As God again awakened the gospel of pure and precious grace in the Reformation through his servant Martin Luther, he led Luther through the monastery. . . .
> Luther's way out of the monastery into the world carried the sharpest attack which was made on the world since the time of the Early Church.[20]

From 1936 to 1946 the element of "this-sidedness," of "worldliness," grew more and more explicit, but it was present also in his most world-denying early writings. He was prepared to defend the secret spiritual life of the Christians, the *disciplina arcana*, but the accent on the "worldly exposition" of the gospel was undisguised throughout: "Only he who cries out for the Jews may also sing Gregorian [chant]." [21]

The Church and the World

Bonhoeffer's approach was, therefore, relatively consistent. The very emphasis upon the church, her recovery of discipline, her secret spiritual life, her repudiation of accommodation, was bound closely to her mission in the world. He was loyal to the anti-Nazi Barmen Confession (1934) and among other things to its First and Second Articles:

> Jesus Christ, as he is testified to us in the Holy Scripture, is the one Word of God, whom we are to hear, whom we are to trust and obey in life and in death.
>
> We repudiate the false teaching that the church can and must recognize yet other happenings and powers, images and truths as divine revelation alongside this one Word of God, as a source of her preaching.
>
> Just as Jesus Christ is the pledge of the forgiveness of all our sins, just so—and with the same earnestness—is he also God's mighty claim on our whole life; in him we encounter a joyous liberation from the godless claims of this world to free and thankful service to his creatures.
>
> We repudiate the false teaching that there are areas of our life in which we belong not to Jesus Christ but another lord, areas in which we do not need justification and sanctification through him.[22]

These rigorous and exclusive claims were not, however, put forward to justify any pietistic or sectarian view of the church. No continuing city was to be erected here, as a kind of ecclesiastical fortress amidst the stormy vicissitudes of history. Later, writing from prison, Bonhoeffer criticized a restorationist tendency which he detected in the Confessing Church.[23] The whole notion of "clearing a space for religion in the world or against the world" was wrongheaded. In August of 1944, in an outline he sketched for a book, he felt that even his friend Karl Barth had become abstract and nonexistential at this point.

Barth and the Confessing Church have encouraged us to entrench ourselves behind the "faith of the Church," and evade the honest question, what is our real and personal belief? Hence lack of fresh air, even in the Confessing Church. To say, "It's the church's faith, not mine," can be a clericalist subterfuge, and outsiders always regard it as such. Much the same applies to the suggestion of the dialectical theologians that we have no control over our faith, and so it is impossible for us to say what we do believe. There may be a place for such considerations, but they do not release us from the duty of being honest with ourselves.[24]

The church is there for the sake of the world, not as an esoteric nest, and the responsibility to communicate was even more a test of true orthodoxy than the structure of internal logic and coherence. "She must tell men, whatever their calling, what it means to live in Christ, to exist for others." [25]

There were two traditional hardened views of the church-world problem, and Bonhoeffer was unwilling to accept either of them. The one against which he reacted first was that of the continuum of Christ and culture, of religious values and secular values, of "the German way of life" and "the Christian way of life," of tribal mores sanctified by a spirituality without biblical integrity. Facing this front, he stressed the biblical note of discontinuity.

It is a theological error of the first magnitude to exploit the doctrine of Christ as the Mediator so as to justify the enjoyment of direct relationships in the things of this world. . . . For the Christian the only God-given realities are those he receives from Christ. What is not given us through the incarnate son is not given us by God.[26]

He had already repudiated the traditional concept of Christendom, as it had become static and was finally to be possessed by demonic, anti-Christian forces, even before Hitler came to power.

Before the war we lived too far from God; we believed too much in our own power, in our almightiness and righteousness. We attempted to be a strong and good people, but we were too proud of our endeavors, we felt too much satisfaction with our scientific, economic and social progress, and we identified this progress with the coming of the Kingdom of God.[27]

The second traditional (and static) way of viewing the church-world problem was the sectarian view, which he commonly identified with Pietism and the free churches, in which the church becomes a kind of heavily walled fortress set in the midst of hostile territory. At first Bonhoeffer seems to have been tempted by the thought of taking the path of the free churches. He had already concluded that church discipline was impossible in the established church: "Excommunication in a *Volkskirche*, because it can't be performed, is senseless." [28] In his correspondence and activities in connection with the Fanö (1934) Conference of the World Alliance for International Friendship Through the Churches it would seem that he expected the universal church to declare and condemn heresy in the official German church.[29] In the same year he encouraged his students to debate the alternatives as to church order, and Franz Hildebrandt put forward "Ten Theses for a Free Church." [30] His efforts to recover the concept of "heresy" and to restore church discipline within the establishment were all fruitless; yet he could not bring himself to accept the free church ("sectarian") solution. It is perhaps at this point that Bonhoeffer showed himself most a child of German Christendom, for, even though he repudiated Ernst Troeltsch's typology of church and sect,[31] he—like most of the men of the Confessing Church—drew his understanding of the free churches primarily from the Pietistic, conventicle-type German "free churches," and identified them with the "fortress concept" of the church. As he had said in the *Nachfolge*, "The disciples of Jesus must not fondly imagine that they can simply run away from the world and huddle together in a little band." [32]

Bonhoeffer's quest was a new statement of the church, not in terms of static pattern—"continuum" or "fortress"—but in terms of her mission to the world. That mission required a certain attention to discipline of theological confession and practical witness. Nor could theology be divorced from action.

> Only now are we Germans beginning to discover the meaning of free responsibility. It depends upon a God who demands bold action as the free response of faith, and who promises forgiveness and consolation to the man who becomes a sinner in the process. [33]

The error of the old orthodoxy had been to slip into irrelevant verbalization. As the Bishop of Chichester put it:

> He quickly realized that in the situation in which the world and the churches found themselves in the 'thirties nothing was gained any longer for the churches by citing their old credal statements. The ecumenical movement seemed to him to offer the only way of reuniting the various members of the body of Christ. This explains why Bonhoeffer considered it the duty of the churches to listen anew to the message of the Bible and to put themselves in the context of the whole church. [34]

With a strong sense of the inadequacy of old patterns of churchmanship, Bonhoeffer looked to the future with faith and hope. Even in prison, he was still confident that the Lord of History had not lost control:

> I feel as curious as the angels in I Peter 1:12 as to how God intends to resolve these apparently insoluble issues. I am sure God is about to do something which we can only accept with wonder and amazement. . . .
>
> The thing that keeps coming back to me is, what is Christianity, and indeed what is Christ, for us to-day? The time when men could be told everything by means of words, whether theological or simply pious, is over, and

so is the time of inwardness and conscience, which is to say the time of religion as such. We are proceeding towards a time of no religion at all: men as they are now simply cannot be religious any more. Our whole nineteen-hundred-year-old Christian preaching and theology rests upon the "religious premise" of man. What we call Christianity has always been a pattern—perhaps a true pattern —of religion. But if one day it becomes apparent that this a priori "premise" simply does not exist, but was an historical and temporary form of human self-expression, i.e. if we reach the stage of being radically without religion— and I think this is more or less the case already, else how is it, for instance, that this war, unlike any of those before it, is not calling forth any "religious" reaction?—what does that mean for "Christianity"?

It means that the linchpin is removed from the whole structure of our Christianity to date. . . . (April 30, 1944) [35]

In his search for a clear interpretation of the nature of the crisis, in striving to find a new and dynamic understanding of the church-world problem, Bonhoeffer was thus moved to a new statement of the periodization of Church History. The church was to be understood in terms of mission rather than pattern. The exciting age of Church History was neither the sixteenth century nor the fourth century, not the Middle Ages nor even the Early Church (although the latter period retained a certain normative significance): the golden age of the church lay directly before, when the church should die like her Lord to the redemption of the world. The new task of the church was not to save her own life, nor even primarily to face down the persecutor: it was to go out of the temple into the world of workers, citizens, civil servants, business men, scientists.

The World Come of Age

Bonhoeffer believed that the world had passed into a post-religious phase. He was thinking, of course, primarily of a Europe ravaged by two world wars, two types of totalitarianism, two major depressions.[36] "Surely there has never been a generation in the course of human history with so little ground under its feet as our own." [37] But the process of secularization had not been a sudden one: it had begun long before with Lord Herbert of Cherbury, Machiavelli, and others at the beginning of the "modern age."

> In natural science the process seems to start with Nicolas of Cusa and Giordano Bruno with their "heretical" doctrine of the infinity of space. The classical cosmos was finite, like the created world of the middle ages. An infinite universe, however it be conceived, is self-subsisting *etsi deus non daretur*. . . . There is no longer any need for God as a working hypothesis, whether in morals, politics or science. Nor is there any need for such a God in religion or philosophy (Feuerbach). In the name of intellectual honesty these working hypotheses should be dropped or dispensed with as far as possible. (July 16, 1944)[38]

On the other hand, the process of secularization was by no means a purely negative one: implied in it is the taking over of Christian truth by the world. It is only from within the defensive lines of the church, from within a protectionist view of the church, that such secularization is resented and feared.

> The attack by Christian apologetic upon the adulthood of the world I consider to be in the first place pointless, in the second ignoble, and in the third un-Christian.[39]

The incarnational theology affords the clue to his lack of restraint toward the world, even toward natural impulses which a resolute ascetic would view with suspicion.

> The Christian, unlike the devotees of the salvation myths, does not need a last refuge in the eternal from earthly tasks and difficulties. But like Christ himself ("My God, my God, why hast thou forsaken me?") he must drink the earthly cup to the lees, and only in his doing that is the crucified and risen Lord with him, and he crucified and risen with Christ. This world must not be prematurely written off. In this the Old and New Testaments are at one. Myths of salvation arise from human experiences of the boundary situation. Christ takes hold of a man in the center of his life. (June 27, 1944) [40]

The incarnate and redeeming Christ was not confined to the body of the church. The problem was to break out of the protectionist posture.

> In what way are we in a religionless and secular sense Christians, in what way are we the *Ekklesia*, "Those who are called forth," not conceiving of ourselves religiously as specially favoured, but as wholly belonging to the world? Then Christ is no longer an object of religion, but something quite different, in deed and in truth the Lord of the world. (April 30, 1944) [41]

A radical theology of Incarnation will not stop with discipleship, or even with the church as the mystical body of Christ. It moves on to an awareness of the worldly and the purely human which are made new in Him who is both redeemer and creator.

It is significant that Bonhoeffer should have arrived at the materialism of the Old Testament by way of the Christ.

> Unlike the other oriental religions the faith of the Old Testament is not a religion of salvation. Christianity, it is true, has always been regarded as a religion of salvation. But isn't this a cardinal error, which divorces Christ from the Old Testament and interprets him in the light of the myths of salvation? . . . The Old Testament speaks of *historical* redemption, i.e. redemption on this side of

death, whereas the myths of salvation are concerned to
offer men deliverance from death. Israel is redeemed out
of Egypt in order to live before God on earth. (June 27,
1944) [42]

There is no purely spiritual redemption of the individual apart
from this world. Bonhoeffer's attention to the historical, the
material, the concrete, led him back to the Old Testament
along many paths. On November 28, 1943, he had prepared
an Advent meditation in which he turned again against pure
"inwardness," solitary self-knowledge.

> My thoughts and feelings seem to be getting more and
> more like the Old Testament, and no wonder, I have been
> reading it more than the New for the last few months. It
> is only when one knows the ineffability of the Name of
> God that one can utter the name of Jesus Christ. It is
> only when one loves life and the world so much that with-
> out them everything would be gone, that one can believe
> in the resurrection and a new world. It is only when one
> submits to the law that one can speak of grace, and only
> when one sees the anger and wrath of God hanging like
> grim realities over the head of one's enemies that one can
> know something of what it means to love them and for-
> give them. I don't think it is Christian to want to get to
> the New Testament too soon and too directly. [43]

If he is truly the redeemer, the giver of life, then God is
central and not death and sin. For the theological man (that
is, the Christian man thinking), the Pietist moment of inward
struggle and turning again cannot be normal: rather the normal is the life of the New Man in the New Creation.

> I should like to speak of God not on the borders of life
> but as its centre, not in weakness but in strength, not,
> therefore, in man's suffering and death but in his life and
> prosperity. . . . The church stands not where human pow-
> ers give out, on the borders, but in the centre of the vil-
> lage. That is the way it is in the Old Testament, and in

this sense we still read the New Testament far too little on the basis of the Old. (April 30, 1944) [44]

The world which had come of age was no longer addressed by a purely spiritual message. For a time the words and the institutions which functioned in this context may have communicated something. But the autonomous world of the modern age was no longer able or willing to hear such a gospel. The introspective bent of a degenerate spirituality had become positively indecent.[45] Among mature persons there should be a certain reticence about the *pudenda* and about the state of one's soul. Certainly the awful lack of privacy in prison life had helped him to see this point more clearly.

> In short I know less than ever about myself, and am getting more and more bored with psychology and fed up with introspective analysis. . . . There is something more at stake than self-knowledge. (December 15, 1943)[46]
>
> Is it not true to say that individualistic concern for personal salvation has almost completely left us all? Are we not really under the impression that there are more important things than bothering about such a matter? . . . Is there any concern in the Old Testament about saving one's soul at all? . . . It is not with the next world that we are concerned, but with this world as created and preserved and set subject to laws and atoned for and made new. What is above the world is, in the Gospel, intended to exist for this world. . . . (May 5, 1944)[47]

The New Man

It is a moving and liberating experience to read the modest, human references in the letters from prison. As the comfort of family and children's voices were denied him, the correspondence and occasional visits of friends became more precious. It was not that having abandoned "the attachments of this world" he was not free to "justify the enjoyment of direct

relationships with the things of this world." [48] Rather, another
form of words would do him more justice: living in anticipation of the last things, suffering desperately from time to time
from homesickness, he laid strong hold of the personal relationships which alone were real in life. "To be a Christian
therefore means for Bonhoeffer not to be 'religious' in a certain way, but to be truly human." [49] To be truly human means
to live under the hand of Him who makes all things new, by
whom all worlds are made, and by whom this broken world is
redeemed and remade.

> What does "bring again" mean? It means that nothing is
> lost, everything is taken up again in Christ, though of
> course it is transfigured in the process, becoming trans-
> parent, clear and free from all self-seeking and desire.
> Christ brings it all again as God intended it to be. . . .[50]

What *tone* is to the musician, the *view of the person* is to
the Christian.[51] At no point is the relation with persons abstract: it remains a face-to-face encounter. Thus Bonhoeffer
wrote in *Sanctorum Communio*—

> My real relationship to other persons is controlled by
> my relationship to God. Just as however I first know
> God's "I" in the revelation of His love, so also [I know]
> other people; here the view of the church is involved.[52]
> The Christian concept of person is conceived histori-
> cally, that is in its condition after the fall; for history in
> the genuine historical sense begins first with sin and the
> related destination to death.[53]

Writing from prison, in acceptance of his situation and in acceptance of others, he held to and deepened the this-sidedness
of the relationship.

> So long as we are suffering from an exaggerated sense of
> our own importance we can never really love our neigh-
> bors: love of one's neighbor remains something vague
> and abstract. Today I am able to take a calmer view of

other people, of their needs and responsibilities, and so
I am able to help them more.[54]

He wrote of dependence on others and his gratitude for them.
He longed repeatedly for reunion with friends and family, and
wrote feelingly of shared experiences in the past. "One thing
is that I do miss sitting down to table with others" (November
21, 1943).[55] In "A Wedding Sermon" (May, 1943) he wrote
movingly of home:

> Most people have forgotten nowadays what a home can
> mean, though some of us have come to realize it as never
> before. . . . It is an ordinance God has established in the
> world, the place where peace, quietness, joy, love, purity,
> continence, respect, obedience, traditions, and, to crown
> them all, happiness may dwell, whatever else may pass
> away in the world.[56]

He found excitement in good books, in flowers, in that little
fragment of nature which crept into the prison year (a bird's
nest!), in food and little luxuries. He was inordinately grateful
for cigars ("my favorite Wolf cigars from Hamburg") left
him by Karl Barth and W. A. Visser't Hooft after a visit in
November, 1943.[57] He discussed frankly the old Prussian ethic,
iron discipline, and moralism which so often restricted the area
of freedom and made difficult a spontaneous response to
friendship, music, and games.[58] "I am sure we honour God
more if we gratefully accept the life he gives us with all its
blessings. . . ."[59] Bonhoeffer did not want to slide into the
vulgar cult of "the human"—the sentimentalization of folksy
ways so familiar in Communist poetry and films. "What I
mean, however, is the simple fact that people are more important in life than anything else."[60]

To be sure, he did on occasion—in spite of his own warnings
to himself of the danger of prison sentimentality—slip into a
romanticizing mood. He approached this danger in writing to
his parents to contrast the fragmentariness of his generation's

life with the "full scope in professional and private activities" which had blessed their own.[61] He fell into it, briefly, in writing as a primitivist of rural life in his "Thoughts on the Baptism of D. W. R." (May, 1944):

> It would be much the best thing if you were brought up in the country. . . . The Bible tells us that Cain was the first city dweller. . . . The tranquility and remoteness of country life . . . the totalitarian claims of city life . . .[62]

But these were rare moments. For the most part he held with consistency to the concrete realities, to a faith worked out within the "given things." In one letter, dated May 20, 1944, he worked out a polyphonic scheme for relating love of God to love of friends.

> What I mean is that God requires that we should love him eternally with our whole hearts, yet not so as to compromise or diminish our earthly affections, but as a kind of *cantus firmus* to which the other melodies of life provide the counterpoint. Earthly affection is one of these contrapuntal themes. . . .[63]

More and more disenchanted by religiosity ("positive thinking"!), he became equally frank in stating his dislikes and negative judgments. He will not agree with Diogenes that the ultimate good is absence of desire: "Why should we pretend that all our geese are swans?" [64] He was impatient at first at the delays in calling up his trial case, in processing his release: "We Christians need not be ashamed of showing a little impatience, longing and discontent with an unnatural fate, nor with a considerable amount of longing for freedom, earthly happiness and opportunity for work." [65] ". . . there is a concern for the blessing of God, which includes all earthly blessings as well." [66] He dressed down a cowardly "German Christian" now whining and ostentatiously "suffering." [67] "Too much altruism is a bore, and makes too many claims." [68] It is clear that Bonhoeffer, even though he had afterthoughts about his treatment of the German Christian, found a certain freedom in personal relations while in prison.

Summing Up

Bonhoeffer never shifted from his early vision of the Christ as redeemer and creator. This view of the Incarnate Lord, expressed in different ways, had revolutionary implications for the concept of the church—which shared her Lord's mission—and for the view of history and the view of the world. In the main, although the touchstone of his thought comes into fairly clear focus, the word about the church, history, and the world is chiefly critical. He exposed and repudiated relentlessly the prevailing errors; the areas of possibility he opened up remained largely unexplored, due to the brevity of his life, and will doubtless remain a subject of discussion for some time to come.

In his message to his namesake he spoke of the way in which the church had failed her Lord, making inevitable a radical change in time to come.

> During these years the Church has fought for self-preservation as though it were an end in itself, and has thereby lost its chance to speak a word of reconciliation to mankind and the world at large. . . . By the time you are grown up, the form of the Church will have changed beyond recognition.[69]

The church cannot live in the world as a tiny fortress, preserving the ancient landmarks and maintaining the righteousness of a tidy minority. Neither can it, with a gospel couched in unintelligible language, speak to a world which "gets along without 'God,' and just as well as before." [70] He praised Karl Barth for having begun the criticism of religion, but criticized his retreating behind a positivist doctrine of revelation.[71] Even though he criticized Rudolf Bultmann's approach as "really at bottom the liberal one (that is, abridging the gospel)," the

significant point is that he thought a far more radical approach
was necessary:

> I expect you remember Bultmann's paper on the demy-
> thologizing of the New Testament. My view of it today
> would be not that he went too far, as most people seem
> to think, but that he did not go far enough.[72]

It is the religious conceptions themselves which must be done
away with. The process of demythologizing Church History,
of exposing the ideational-apologetic style in which it has been
presented and even periodized, would have excited Bonhoeffer's interest and comment.

God's love for the world remained the subject of Bonhoeffer's meditation. If the world were so loved, as the incarnation
showed it to be, then the gospel must communicate to it and
the church must be geared to its service. Neither a sterile orthodoxy nor a self-justifying church fits into God's purpose for
the world.

> The God who makes us live in the world without using
> him as a working hypothesis is the God before whom we
> are ever standing. . . . God allows himself to be edged
> out of the world and on to the cross. . . . Matthew 8:17
> makes it crystal clear that it is not by his omnipotence
> that Christ helps us, but by his weakness and suffering.[73]

Although Bonhoeffer's form of words was frequently revolutionary, therefore, it remains clear that his purpose was in fact
to "work out a non-religious interpretation of biblical terminology." [74] The basic question remained: "How can we reclaim
for Christ a world which has come of age?" [75] That Christ is
not, however, the picture-book savior of the nineteenth century: He is the one who, revealing the face of the God of the
Bible, "conquers power and space in the world by his weakness." [76] He is the Crucified One of this age, too, at the hands
of spiritual men even more than at the hands of the secular-
minded.

Notes for Essay 2

1 Rudolf Pfister, "Le Message de Dietrich Bonhoeffer," 56 *Foi et Vie* (1958) 1:24-33, 33.

2 In John Doberstein's introduction to *Life Together* (New York: Harper & Brothers, 1954), p. 8.

3 *Sanctorum Communio* (Munich: Chr. Kaiser Verlag, 1954), p. 90.

4 *Ibid.*, p. 52.

5 *Ibid.*, p. 93.

6 *Ibid.*, p. 104.

7 *The Cost of Discipleship* (London: Student Christian Movement, 1948), p. 185.

8 *Life Together* (op. cit.), p. 26.

9 Dietrich Bonhoeffer, *Life Together*, John Doberstein, tr. (New York: Harper & Brothers, 1954), p. 38. All other excerpts from *Life Together* in this essay are used by permission.

10 Students of totalitarian ideology frequently use the phrase and make the analogy to Gnosticism; see Eric Voegelin, *The New Science of Politics* (Chicago: University of Chicago Press, 1952); also J. L. Talmon, *The Origins of Totalitarian Democracy* (London: Secker & Warburg, 1952); and Hans Buchheim, *Glaubenskrise im Dritten Reich* (Stuttgart: Deutsche Verlags-Anstalt, 1953).

11 *Creation and Fall: A Theological Interpretation of Genesis 1-3*, John C. Fletcher, tr. (New York: The Macmillan Company, 1959), p. 8.

12 *Sanctorum Communio* (op. cit.), p. 164.

13 *Life Together* (op. cit.), p. 37.

14 Reprinted with the permission of the publisher from *The Cost of Discipleship*, pp. 97, 147, by Dietrich Bonhoeffer. Translated by Reginald Fuller. 2nd Rev. Ed. Copyright 1959 by The Macmillan Company. All other excerpts from *The Cost of Discipleship* in this essay are used by permission.

15 *Prisoner for God: Letters and Papers from Prison* (New York: The Macmillan Company, 1957), p. 168.

16 *Life Together* (op. cit.), p. 50.

17 *Prisoner for God* (op. cit.), p. 85.

18 Introduction to the English edition of the *Nachfolge: The Cost of Discipleship*, pp. 24-25.

19 Heinz Zahrnt, "Der Gefangene von Tegel," *Sonntagsblatt* (10 April, 1955), No. 15, p. 1.

20 *The Cost of Discipleship (op. cit.)*, pp. 37f.

21 Quoted in Heinz Zahrnt *(loc. cit.)*, p. 1.

22 Translation in Franklin H. Littell, *The German Phoenix* (New York: Doubleday & Co., Inc. 1960), Appendix B; historical discussion, Ch I.

23 *Prisoner for God (op. cit.)*, p. 148. Following Barmen, the Confessing Church had moved—at its second synod, Dahlem (1935)—directly into questions of church law and sound institutional claims and prerogatives. Does the most meaningful line of communication run from Barmen to Dahlem to Bad Oeynhausen to Augsburg, or directly from Barmen to the Stuttgart Declaration of Guilt? See Franklin H. Littell, "From Barmen (1934) to Stuttgart (1945): The Path of the Confessing Church in Germany," III A *Journal of Church and State* (1961) 1: 41-52.

24 *Prisoner for God (op. cit.)*, p. 180.

25 *Ibid.*

26 *The Cost of Discipleship (op. cit.)*, p. 81.

27 From an address in New York, in the fall of 1930; *Gesammelte Schriften, I: Okumene . . . 1928-1942* (Munich: Chr. Kaiser Verlag, 1958), 69. By permission of the publisher.

28 *Sanctorum Communio (op. cit.)*, p. 196n.

29 *Gesammelte Schriften (op. cit.)*, I, 242f.

30 *Gesammelte Schriften (op. cit.)*, II: *Kirchenkampf und Finkenwalde . . . 1933-1943*, p. 167.

31 *Sanctorum Communio (op. cit.)*, pp. 205f.

32 *The Cost of Discipleship (op. cit.)*, p. 163.

33 *Prisoner for God (op. cit.)*, p. 17.

34 Introduction to *The Cost of Discipleship (op. cit.)*, p. 12.

35 *Prisoner for God (op. cit.)*, pp. 121-122.

36 American Protestantism is still lodged somewhat securely in the nineteenth century, and its situation may be that of existence in a pluralistic society which is "post-Protestant"; it is not "post-Christian" in the European sense. "Two depressions": Germany suffered a major depression and inflation in the period 1921-1924.

37 *Prisoner for God (op. cit.)*, p. 13.

38 *Ibid.*, pp. 162-163.

39 *Ibid.*, p. 147.

40 *Ibid.*, p. 154.

41 *Ibid.*, p. 123.

42 *Ibid.*, p. 153.

43 *Ibid.*, p. 79.

44 *Ibid.*, p. 124.

45 *Ibid.*, pp. 80, 103.

46 *Ibid.* (Dec. 15, 1943), p. 82.

47 *Ibid.* (May 5, 1944), pp. 125-126.

48 *The Cost of Discipleship (op. cit.)*, pp. 73, 81. Supra, ftn. 26.

49 Heinz Zahrnt *(loc. cit.)*, p. 1.

50 "Advent IV," in *Prisoner for God (op. cit.)*, p. 87.

51 *Sanctorum Communio (op. cit.)*, p. 26.

52 *Ibid.*, p. 33.

53 *Ibid.*, p. 36.
54 *Prisoner for God (op. cit.)*, p. 120.
55 *Ibid.*, p. 73.
56 *Ibid.*, p. 37.
57 *Ibid.*, p. 74.
58 *Ibid.* (Jan. 23, 1944), p. 94.
59 *Ibid.*, p. 93.
60 *Ibid.* (Aug. 10, 1944), p. 182.
61 *Ibid.* (Feb. 20, 1944), p. 61; also (Feb. 23, 1944), pp. 105-106.
62 *Ibid.*, p. 136.
63 *Ibid.*, p. 131.
64 *Ibid.* (Oct. 4, 1943), p. 52.
65 *Ibid.* (Nov. 15, 1943), p. 66.
66 *Ibid.* (July 28, 1944), p. 173.
67 *Ibid.* (Feb. 2, 1944), p. 100.
68 *Ibid.* (May 6, 1944), p. 127.
69 *Ibid.* (May, 1944), p. 140.
70 *Ibid.* (June 8, 1944), p. 146.
71 *Ibid.* (May 5, 1944), p. 126.
72 *Ibid.*, p. 125.
73 *Ibid.* (July 16, 1944), p. 164.
74 *Ibid.*, p. 162.
75 *Ibid.* (June 30, 1944), p. 157.
76 *Ibid.* (July 16, 1944), p. 164.

3

The Social Character of the Question
Concerning Jesus Christ

Elsewhere Peter Berger has written that "in our situation there is a special call for . . . intellectual toughness in being willing to perceive the social reality of religion. It may well be that the decisive skandalon for Christian commitment in our time is precipitated not by history or biology or psychology but by sociology." By "our situation" he means the social innocence of the Church comfortably established in the Western world. Professor Berger looks for this intellectual toughness in dealing with the empirical church in the earliest writing of Dietrich Bonhoeffer and finds it largely lacking. In this view, Bonhoeffer took a poorer choice between two alternative schools of German social thought at the time. Another way of putting it is this: in the essay Sanctorum Communio, "a systematic inquiry into the sociology of the Church," the young theologian set out to stress the concreteness of revelation in Jesus Christ in the Church, but used incongruous abstract tools.

Despite this methodological fault, there is much merit in the early work. It prefigures many of Bonhoeffer's last concerns in the prison letters and refutes the idea of a real breach in his early and late work. The intent of the essay imposed an almost impossible problem on Bonhoeffer: how to take seriously the kind of "intellectual toughness" associated with names like Ernst Troeltsch or his own teacher, Adolf Harnack, in dealing with the Church's visibility—and at the same time how to do justice to the transcendent note in the theology of revelation which we associate with names like Karl Barth in that period.

The Church is "Christ existing as community"—a thoroughly concrete and literally vivid picture. If this early view sees Christ to be "the man for others" in the Church and the final view sees him to be "the man for others" in the world, yet the basic movement, the basic shape of action from God toward man is already predetermined.

The reader who is having his first contact with the thought of Bonhoeffer would do well to postpone reading the analyses of the early works in the following two essays until he has finished the rest of the book. Those familiar with much of his thought will, however, do well to see these ideas in their chronological and systematic context, as they are located here. Those who do not pursue the disciplines of sociology or religion will be interested to find here clues to the reasons why Bonhoeffer was not concerned at this time with basic structural change in the Church. They may also be alerted to his criticism of the small groups which have become vogues in the Church today. They will certainly feel judged by Professor Berger's criticism of the quest for concreteness in revelation through inadequate and abstract analytical tools.

Professor Berger is now with the Hartford Seminary Foundation. The author of The Noise of Solemn Assemblies, the Viennese-born thinker lauds Bonhoeffer as a prophet of intellectual toughness in the modern world in his most recent book, The Precarious Vision.

Sociology and Ecclesiology

By Peter Berger

SINCE the end of World War II the interest in the work of
Dietrich Bonhoeffer has been growing steadily on both sides of
the Atlantic, both in theological circles proper and among
those whose relationship to theology is less than professional.
Fortunately or unfortunately, however one may look at it,
Bonhoeffer's thought is very difficult to systematize, if only
because it was so intimately bound up with the violent events
confronting him as a thinker fully engaged in the moral and
political questions of his time. Bonhoeffer wrote his works in
response to very different situations. It is inevitable then that
quite different theological positions are presented today as
being somehow legitimated in Bonhoeffer's thought.

Those who contend that the main event of recent Christian
history has been the rediscovery of the Church will emphasize
Bonhoeffer's extensive articles and correspondence about the
ecumenical movement. Those concerned with the political and
social responsibility of Christians will look to Bonhoeffer's
involvement in the German resistance movement, and will
find inspiration in the courageous determination of such works
as *The Cost of Discipleship*. Those with a stake in devotional
experiments can appeal to *Life Together*. And those looking
for radical new postures of the Christian in the modern world
will naturally concentrate on *Ethics* and the letters now entitled *Prisoner for God*. Something like this will happen, of

course, to every thinker who somehow captures the imagination of a generation, often in ways that the members of this generation cannot themselves articulate clearly. In Bonhoeffer's case the problem is more acute because the time was not given to him to integrate the various strands of his thought into a coherent theological system.

His work on the sociology of the Church, *Sanctorum Communio*, has not as yet been subjected to this process of appeal and identification.[1] At the time of writing, no English translation of the book exists, although a brief summary is available in John Godsey's study of Bonhoeffer's theology.[2] In any event, the pedantic style and highly technical content of much of the book will likely hold off the enthusiasts, even if they reflect upon the sad truth (all too evident in this instance) that academic dissertations are not written to enlighten the public but to impress a faculty committee. Bonhoeffer was 21 years old when he submitted *Sanctorum Communio* as a dissertation to the theological faculty of the University of Berlin. The dissertation was accepted in 1927, and Bonhoeffer was awarded his licentiate in theology. *Sanctorum Communio* was published as a book in 1930, just before Bonhoeffer's departure for his first period of study in the United States. A new publication of this edition came out in Germany in 1954.

If *Sanctorum Communio* should be headed for more attention by theologians and theologically interested persons on this side of the Atlantic, it is likely to be the subtitle rather than the title that will first attract this attention—"Dogmatic Investigation on the Sociology of the Church." The word sociology has been a trigger for emotional response to American theologians before. For old-line liberals "sociology" (sometimes with the qualifying adjective "Christian" before it) was, so to speak, the secular arm of the Social Gospel. For the neo-orthodox it frequently became an intellectual whipping post to which were to be tied all the things supposed to be wrong with liberal theology. Today there is some evidence that as neo-orthodoxy has come to be something less than the latest vogue, there is renewed interest among theologians in the possible contribution to their task by the social sciences. If this interest should itself become a new fashion, Bonhoeffer's *Sanctorum Communio* would seem to be a natural choice for a legitimating classic. We shall briefly consider whether this work of Bonhoeffer's could provide us with a foundation for the dialogue between theology and the social sciences, especially insofar as the latter deal with the same phenomena that concern ecclesiology. We shall avoid the temptation of searching the argument of *Sanctorum Communio* for the ideas that came to fruition years later in Bonhoeffer's thought. We shall rather consider the work by itself and in terms of its own problematic.

Godsey tells us that Karl Barth called *Sanctorum Communio* a "theological miracle." [3] This somewhat startling statement can be understood only if we see the work against the background of the theological climate of opinion in Germany in the late 1920's.[4] This was the period when the new dialectical theology (the same general movement that came later to be called neo-orthodoxy in America) had established itself as the dominant wave among the younger generation of theologians. Despite great differences between their several approaches to theology, there was a common frame of reference uniting the theologians that came to the fore in this wave—Karl Barth, Emil Brunner, Eduard Thurneysen, Friedrich Gogarten, and Rudolf Bultmann. Along with the rejection of the old liberal individualism came a new ecclesiological concern. This was expressed not only within the circle of dialectical theology properly speaking. The renascence of a strongly confessional, self-conscious Lutheranism, expressed in the work of men like Paul Althaus and Werner Elert, contributed to this concern.

About the same time came the birth of a High Church movement in Germany, centered in the Berneuchener Circle of Wilhelm Staehlin and expressing itself in a vigorous liturgical revival. Even the appearance of a new religious socialism, then associated with the name of Paul Tillich, can be seen in connection with this reawakened concern for the Christian community as it exists in the real, empirical world. Recalling once more the date of the original writing of *Sanctorum Communio*, it is relevant to glance at some of the dates just preceding it in this development: 1919—publication of Barth's *Epistle to the Romans*; 1923—founding of the periodical "Between the Times" (*Zwischen den Zeiten*), which served as a focus for the entire group of dialectical theologians; 1926—publication of Tillich's *The Religious Situation of the Present*; and also in 1926—founding of the periodical "Berneuchener Book" by the Staehlin group.

One important element that united the new theologians as against both the old liberals and the old conservatives was the dialectical tension that gave its name to their thought. Crudely put, it was the tension between an essentially nonrational affirmation of faith in the contents of Christian orthodoxy on the one hand, and a cheerful surrender to rational-scientific analysis in matters of biblical criticism, church history, religious psychology, and all other aspects of natural religion on the other hand. As the first aspect of this tension separated the new theologians from the old liberals, so the second aspect set them aside from the old conservatives. This tension expressed itself in almost any theological problem that was to be tackled. It is easy to see how it would manifest itself in the ecclesiological area. Here the tension would have to be between the dogmatic affirmation of the communion of saints and the acceptance of the empirical reality, in history and society, and even in the individual psyche, in which this communion appears to the rational mind. On the one hand: "communion of saints," "body of Christ," "mystery of the Church." On the other hand: historical causality, social processes, psychological patterns. This dialectic was resolved in different ways by the theologians of the time. The problem was common to all of them.

Bonhoeffer's *Sanctorum Communio* is an attempt at confronting this dialectic in its social dimension. Other works had already done so with regard to the historical and psychological dimensions. In common with these it has to find a solution to the problem of revelation occurring within an empirical world subject to scientific understanding. Among the previous questions were such as these: "How can revelation occur in historical forms?" "What is the relationship between the Church of Christian faith and the endlessly changing ecclesiastical institutions found in history?" "Can Christian faith be understood other than in terms of man's psychological needs?" The question to which Bonhoeffer here addresses himself is similar in form (which is the dialectic) but different in content: "How can the Church, as the communion of saints, exist empirically as a social institution?" This is the central problematic of the book.

Sanctorum Communio begins with definitions of the fields of social philosophy and sociology.[5] These, of course, are the areas within which Bonhoeffer's dogmatic investigation is to enter into dialogue. As often, the definitions given at the beginning of an argument foreshadow the lines to be followed later. It may then be worthwhile to look closely at these definitions.

Bonhoeffer urges that the two disciplines be kept sharply distinct, although both are cultural sciences, logically different from the natural sciences. Social philosophy is defined as the analysis of the ultimate nature of social relations, their origin and essence in terms of the human spirit. Social philosophy thus precedes any empirical findings about society and must always serve as a corrective for sociology. The latter, on the other hand, is defined as the science of the structure of empirical collectivities. Thus far, at any rate, few sociologists will quarrel with Bonhoeffer, though philosophers of different schools might rebel. To take the empirical as the *differentia* between the two disciplines is in agreement with the sociological tradition since its inception. But if one looks further at what Bonhoeffer means by sociology as an empirical discipline, more dubious aspects of his definition emerge.

Bonhoeffer emphasizes that sociology is concerned with social structure on a very high level of abstraction. Thus sociology is not a historical but a systematic discipline. Its method Bonhoeffer describes as phenomenological, meaning by this the grasp of the essential elements to be found in any empirical data about society. Bonhoeffer then explicitly rejects not only the "morphological-descriptive" sociology of the French school of Emile Durkheim, but also Max Weber's understanding of sociology as a historical discipline. Thus he calls it hardly understandable that Weber should speak of sociology when he studies the complex historical interrelationships of politics, economics, and religion. It follows, of course, that sociology will use this same phenomenological method in studying religion and religious institutions.

Bonhoeffer's concept of sociology is taken from the so-called formalistic school, then quite prominent in Germany. Its most important figure at the time was Georg Simmel, though Bonhoeffer's other main witnesses fall into the same general category (sometimes also called "systematic sociology")—Ferdinand Toennies, Alfred Vierkandt, Theodor Litt.[6] This is not the place to discuss the relative merits and weaknesses of this school as compared with the Weberian approach to sociology that became the dominant one in Germany. What is important for us, however, is *what this choice of definition does to Bonhoeffer's argument.*

The formalists in sociology were anxious to safeguard a very high and distinctive level of abstraction for their discipline. In theory, as is also the case with Bonhoeffer, they retained a concept of sociology as an empirical discipline. In practice, however, the level of abstraction on which they operated became constantly blurred with the level of abstraction of philosophy. That is, their contention that they were engaged in something empirical was precarious at most times. A scholar of Simmel's caliber was able to make the fine distinctions necessary to preserve this contention. Lesser lights, however, could not do so. The rejection of historical data as the real stuff of sociological analysis thus led very easily to speculative systemizing that had little to do with empirical data of any kind.

Bonhoeffer's appropriation of formalistic sociology falls prey from the beginning to this danger. The empirical is retained as an element of definition. But one looks in vain through the pages of *Sanctorum Communio* for any utilization of empirical data concerning the relationship of religion and society. In other words, despite Bonhoeffer's definitions, his dialogue is actually one between social philosophy and dogmatic theology, both operating on levels of abstraction safely removed from the harshness of empirical data. Let it be quickly said that this does not necessarily invalidate the rest of the argument. But, from the beginning, it puts a serious question mark behind Bonhoeffer's claim to provide a theological answer to the problem of the sociology of religion.

In line with this *a priori* approach, Bonhoeffer sets up his basic concept of the person, which he maintains to be the basis of any understanding of society.[7] After briefly discussing a number of alternate concepts from the history of philosophy, Bonhoeffer arrives at what he regards as the specifically Christian concept of the person. The person originates in and passes away again in time. Ultimately, the person can be understood only in the relationship to divine transcendence. But even within the temporal process the person essentially and inevitably requires the existence of others. Personality is always being toward others, in relation with others, confronting others in social situations. Bonhoeffer's person is an "ethical-social reflexive concept."[8] Therefore, the heart of the Christian concept of the person is responsibility. Man is profoundly social and hence, in his essence, a responsible being. Society cannot be understood except as a web of mutually responsive and responsible beings. "The fundamental category of the social is the I/Thou relationship." [9] But, for Christian thought, this relationship cannot be understood in merely immanent terms. It is God who wills the person and it is God's Holy Spirit that enters into each human confrontation. This occurs, presumably, even among men who are quite oblivious of this divine presence. It is only through God's revelation of Himself that men can become conscious of the meaning of divine love. It is, therefore, in the Christian community that the fullness of personality can be realized. Here is the point of origin of Bonhoeffer's ecclesiology.

Here, once more, we can see Bonhoeffer's thought closely akin (we cannot say how far this is due to direct influence) to philosophical currents of his time. One is strongly reminded of Henri Bergson, Martin Buber, and Max Scheler in various parts of this argumentation.[10] What Bonhoeffer does, in fact, is to cap a certain philosophical approach with a theological extension. This in itself is quite unobjectionable, but it is a little difficult to understand Bonhoeffer's assertion that there is something specifically Christian about this approach. As it is, the dogmatic part of Bonhoeffer's investigation at this point of the argument, as at others, smacks a little of theological imperialism. That is, elements are taken out of other disciplines and pressed willy-nilly into a theological frame of reference. It is open to question whether the kind of dialogue that Bonhoeffer intended to engage in in this book allows this sort of procedure.

Starting from these presuppositions, Bonhoeffer then proceeds to tackle his two principal problems in a theological way—the problem of community in general and then the problem of Christian community, that is, the ecclesiological problem proper. The explication of the first problem consists very largely of a further development of the basic concepts of personality and society already delineated.[11] With the help of various illustrations the case is made stronger that for one to be a person one requires the presence of society. Self-consciousness is possible only in interaction with the consciousness of others. This is already evident in any analysis of the social character of language. And in the same way there can be no will that is not oriented toward the wills of others. Bonhoeffer quotes with approval a formulation by Othmar Spann (another contemporary proponent of systematic sociology): "All spiritual being (Geistigkeit) of man only becomes evident in mutuality. This is the essence of spirit (Geist)—to be oneself through being in the other." [12]

To this point, Bonhoeffer expresses ideas that are well within the general consensus of the most varied schools of sociology. Even the heavily empirical social psychology that developed in America about the time that Bonhoeffer was writing (one may think here of such figures as Charles Cooley, W. I. Thomas, and George H. Mead) would arrive at very similar formulations. But from there Bonhoeffer once more takes off in a direction that removes him pretty far from any empirical sociological thought—namely, in his concept of the "collective person."

In an essentially Hegelian manner (here the argument is especially close to Spann), Bonhoeffer argues that a community can be understood as a collective person with much the same structure that characterizes the individual person. He is careful, however, to make clear that this is not to be understood in terms of some sort of mystic participation of the individual in society. Yet while rejecting this extreme form of organicism in the view of society, Bonhoeffer maintains that the empirical consciousness that denies the reality of social entities over and beyond the individual participants in society must be overcome. Certainly, the collective person is dependent upon the presence of individual persons. But it nevertheless has a being and even a will of its own, a will that may be set over against the wills of individuals. There can even be I/Thou relationships between an individual and a collective person (as, for instance, in personal loyalty to an institution).

The crucial question here, as Bonhoeffer sees quite clearly, is whether such collective persons can command ethical responsibility on the part of individuals. Of course, he answers this question in the affirmative. And here is precisely another danger point in Bonhoeffer's argument (as particularly the development of Hegelian social thought in Germany has shown all too clearly). It is one thing to speak of the independent being of collectivities as an exploratory device for a better understanding of society (as, for example, Durkheim and his followers did). It is quite another thing when these entities (such as "the family," "the nation," "the state") take on the quality of mythological beings that make moral demands over against the imperatives of personal morality.

This very debatable positing of collective persons is then, once more, legitimated by a theological formulation. It is God who, supposedly, thinks of man not as an individual being but as one in constant relations with other men. To quote Bonhoeffer's concise summary of this position:

> God wills not the history of individual men but the history of communities of men. But God does not will a community that absorbs the individual but a community of men. For His regard community and individual are present in the same instant and resting in each other. *Before the eyes of God the structures of collective and individual unity are identical.* On these fundamental relationships rests the concept of the religious community and of the Church.[13]

We shall ask a little later whether this is, indeed, the only way in which Christian ethics and anthropology can look upon social reality. For the moment, we can see here once more

Bonhoeffer's tendency of theological imperialism, incorporating different elements of philosophical thought into a dogmatic framework. Again, we would raise the question whether this procedure allows the claim that it is an expression of a specifically Christian philosophy.

If social entities can be understood as communities of will, then distinctions between them can be made on the basis of the strength of the collective will to be found in them. It is in this way that Bonhoeffer elaborates Toennies' classical distinction between "community" (Gemeinschaft) and "association" (Gesellschaft). It is the closeness and cohesiveness of the collective will that makes for a community, as against the loose relationships of an association. Thus a church or a nation can be a community by the strength of the collective will residing in it. This, of course, is a meaning of Toennies' terms that almost no empirical sociologist would allow.

Bonhoeffer further elaborates this view of society by the use of Hegel's concept of "objective spirit." [14] This concept refers to the strength by which a community, as a collective person, exists over and beyond its individual members. The concept, of course, is closely related to Hegel's general concept of "objectivization." In community the individual confronts himself as something that has become objective, external to himself, a normative order that flows from his own consciousness and yet becomes a regulative principle. Society as "objective spirit" exercises its will over its members. Its strength depends upon the strength of the individual members, but it yet exists separately from them. Once in existence, society as "objective spirit" cannot be done away with either by the individual or by individuals acting together.

Though this, presumably, is true of all forms of social reality, it is only in a community (in Bonhoeffer's version of Toennies' concept) that one can speak of a truly personal character of the objective spirit. And this, of course, has far-reaching ethical consequences: "It is also clear why an 'association' cannot be allowed personal character. Objective spirit is regarded as a means to an end. But a person can never be a means to an end." [15] In other words, the utilitarian and functional character of associations forbids the application of ultimate ethical imperatives to them. But communities are supposed to have personal character over and beyond any functional utility. Therefore one is supposed to regard them also as moral entities, ultimately to be equated ethically with individual persons. It is not without interest to recall at this point that this use of Hegelian concepts in social philosophy was exactly the German ideology against which Marx applied his most violent debunking critiques. Bonhoeffer's essentially pre-Marxian use of Hegelianism locates his thought rather accurately within a long tradition of German conservative ideology. This observation would also go far in explaining Bonhoeffer's choice of sociological mentors.

From a theological point of view, Bonhoeffer then presents the previously given concept of community as always damaged as a result of human sin. Empirical social reality will always be a broken community. This comes curiously close to regarding the Hegelian anthropology as a kind of pre-Fall sociology. Sin has driven man from this sociological Garden of Eden. The Christian understanding of man in society will thus have to occur within the dogma of original sin. Consistently, Bonhoeffer argues that not only is the individual person enmeshed in sin, but so are collective persons. To put it somewhat nastily, we have here a certain collectivization of Lutheran gloom. To quote: "The 'humanity of sin' is One, although it is broken up in many individuals. It is a collective person, although infinitely torn within itself. It is Adam, as every individual is himself and Adam. This doubleness is its essence and it is only resolved through the unity of the new humanity in Christ." [16]

With this stage of the argument we have reached the threshold of Bonhoeffer's ecclesiology proper. The social-philosophical and sociological argument of the first part of the book serves as the foil for the ecclesiological solution that is to follow. Ecclesiology now becomes the rope by which sociology can pull itself out of the gloomy world of broken community. It is in his ecclesiology that Bonhoeffer proceeds to go about his actual dogmatic business and it is here that he would seem to be most original. And it is probably here that we can come closest to understanding Barth's enthusiastic evaluation of this early work.

The fifth chapter of *Sanctorum Communio* (which has as its heading the title of the entire work) begins with the reiterated statement that all the preceding discussion not only pointed toward the ecclesiological problem but cannot be understood except from an ecclesiological viewpoint.[17] What is said before both about community and about its brokenness in sin remains true when we speak about the Church. The ecclesiological problem, stated in classical Lutheran fashion, is the coexistence in time of the communion of saints and the communion of sinners. The unbelievable wonder of the Church is the existence within it of a new form of human relationship. The problem of the Church is the coexistence of this new form with the empirically given forms of religious sociation.

This understanding of the Church in terms of dialectical tension is safeguarded against two typical misunderstandings that distort either the one or the other facet of this tension. The first misunderstanding is a historicizing one. That is, it misunderstands the Church as simply a religious community. Empirical analysis of the Church (say, historical or sociological or perhaps psychological analysis) will then perceive nothing in the Church except the communion of sinners. The Church as communion of saints can never come into the perspective of this approach. The second misunderstanding Bonhoeffer characterizes as a religious one. This is the confusion of the Church with the kingdom of God. Such a view cannot bear any empirical analysis that would show up the imperfections of ecclesiastical institutions existing in history. The Church is viewed as communion of saints only; and its other aspect, that of the communion of sinners, is resolutely refused. Both these approaches avoid the strenuousness of the dialectical view and are, therefore, tempting to the intellect. But both produce serious distortions and must be rejected in a correct dogmatic understanding.

Following a brief résumé of the view of the Church in the New Testament, Bonhoeffer proceeds to explicate what kind of community the Church is to be. Its essence, as is to be expected, is love, the same love that unites God with man through Jesus Christ and that then unites the members of the Christian community. The Church is to be a collective person in the fullest possible sense of the term. Within it the brokenness between the individual and the community is resolved in love, in active life of one for the other, in the readiness of each to take upon himself the joys and sorrows of all the others. As such a community, the Church not only incorporates the reality of original unbrokenness, but is an eschatological foreshadowing of the true destiny of man. Thus the Church becomes the only full realization of all I/Thou relationships.

Here Bonhoeffer closely follows in Luther's footsteps, as in the formulation in these terms of the meaning of intercessory prayer within the Christian community and the ultimate miracle of the Church—that Christians, with full priestly authority, can forgive each other their sins. This, of course, is what Luther meant when he once said that each Christian becomes Christ to each other Christian—not in the sense of a mystical union, but in the wonder of this full realization of mutual love. The Church, understood in this way, is not just a means to an end (say, an institutional means to a religious end—as liberal theologians would have had it). It is an end in itself, bearing within the real presence of Jesus Christ. "To be in Christ" and "to be in the Church" is one and the same thing.

In this self-forgetfulness of love the brokenness of human relationships is healed. But, of course, this does not liberate the Christian from the limitations and evils of a social reality still under the dominion of sin. His relationship to the Church is still in this age based on faith, on believing rather than seeing. Nevertheless, the nature of the Church cannot be understood unless we perceive what only faith can perceive—namely, that the personal unity of the Church is Jesus Christ Himself. The collective person of the Church can never be fully understood merely as an entity based on human wills, as all other social entities can be. It is not human but divine will that constitutes the deepest being of the Church. In other words, the ultimate reality of the Church is its being as the Body of Christ. Thus the Church is not an ideal to be attained, but a reality in which the Christian participates in faith.

So far Bonhoeffer's argument on the Church moves within an essentially Lutheran frame of reference, despite the accentuations provided by the Barthian elements in Bonhoeffer's thought and by the particular social-philosophical position adopted by him in this work. But even if Bonhoeffer rejects the notion that this view of the Church is only an ideal never to be realized within the vicissitudes of history, he knows that the reality into which the Christian enters here in faith is different from the reality that can be perceived empirically. In this too, of course, he can lean heavily on Lutheran ecclesiology and on Luther himself. But insofar as Bonhoeffer's concept of sociology and hence of the sociological problem of the Church includes the empirical, he is forced to ask how these two kinds of reality relate to each other in specifically sociological terms. This he tries to do in the crucial section entitled "The Empirical Form of the Church," a part of the ecclesiological fifth chapter of the book.[18]

In terms of Bonhoeffer's intellectual apparatus this problem

comes to a focus in the question of the relationship of the Holy
Spirit (or the Spirit of Christ) to the communion of saints with
the objective spirit of the empirical religious community. As
an empirical entity, the Church has an objective spirit just as
any other human institution would have. This objective spirit
binds together the wills of the individual members and pre-
serves the tradition of the institution over the generations.
But can this objective spirit be identified with the Spirit of
Christ in the Church? To this question Bonhoeffer gives a
strongly negative reply. The reason for the reply lies at the
heart of his Lutheran ecclesiology. The Church, despite its
being the Body of Christ, also at the same time remains a
collection of sinners. And its objective spirit as a human institution is affected by this sin. This is why Bonhoeffer now feels
constrained to reject the Hegelian concept of the Church as
one of the highest stages of the ascent toward absolute spirit.

The Christian community always remains the Church of
the Word; that is, it can be grasped only in faith—not through
the movements of Hegelian reason. "Spirit," in Hegel's sense,
can never be identified with God's Holy Spirit. Bonhoeffer
quotes with approval the statement of Eugen Rosenstock:
"The spirit is not God. All sociology begins with this bitter insight." [19] "The 'Word,' " adds Bonhoeffer, "is the cliff against
which breaks the idealistic monism of spirit. For the Word
means that there is still sin, that absolute spirit must struggle
for its dominion, that the Church remains the Church of
sinners." [20] Thus the communion of saints appears in history
as weakness, arising and falling anew. At times it may, indeed,
appear in the form of mighty institutions. But, in principle,
"a Council is not holier than one man alone." [21] And it may
happen in the history of the Church that as Augustine said,
the communion of saints was incarnate in only one family
or even one individual. One is tempted here to think of the
one man Elijah, in whom was all Israel as he confronted the
multitudes (and the institution!) of the priests of Baal. But at

all times it is the pervasive fact of sin that forbids us to identify the objective spirit of empirical religious communities, even Christian ones, with the Spirit of Christ present in His Church.

This, however, does not mean that the Spirit of Christ does not relate itself at all to the objective spirit of the Church. This relationship follows necessarily from God's will that the Church should exist in time. Again, we have here in Bonhoeffer's argument a sort of collectivization of Lutheran concepts that originally referred to the individual Christian. In this case, Bonhoeffer applies to his ecclesiology the classical Lutheran dogma of the internal testimony of the Holy Spirit. Just as the Holy Spirit bears the internal testimony of the truth of God's revelation to the individual Christian as he hears the Word, so the Holy Spirit continues to guide, admonish, and instruct the objective spirit of the Christian community in history. And, of course, Bonhoeffer here sharply separates himself from any Catholic concept of the Church. Not only individual Christians but the objective spirit of the Church is liable to sin and error. The historicity of the Church implies an infinity of individual characteristics, accidental constellations, and imperfections. None of these must ever be identified with the Spirit of Christ. But the real presence of Christ continues "in, with, and under" these historical foibles. This presence, however, cannot become an object of rational cognition. It is apparent only through faith.

Toward the end of his ecclesiological chapter, having laid down the dogmatic orientation of his interpretation, Bonhoeffer takes up a number of more practical problems. These must be seen again in terms of the particular German background of the work. There is, above all, the problem of the Church existing in the form of a folk church, rather than in the form of a completely voluntary free church. The answer given to this question is again in the tradition of Lutheran ecclesiology. The Church can exist as folk church because the

Word is addressed to all men. To try to separate the wheat from the chaff in this time of the waiting Church is to pre-empt the end of the age. This, of course, is the classic Lutheran (and, for that matter, orthodox Calvinist) critique of all fanatic attempts to limit the visible Church to the company of the elect. The Church, however, can be a folk church only if the way is always open to the voluntary, free, individual response to the Word of God. If a situation should arise in which this is no longer possible, then the form of the folk church would have lost its theological justification. But in that case the decision to become a free church would have to be based on church-political rather than on dogmatic grounds. This became a burning issue during the German church struggle under the Nazi regime. It is interesting to see Bonhoeffer's clear presentation of the logic endorsed by the theologians of the Confessing Church some six years after *Sanctorum Communio* was written.

Despite this openness toward changes in the form of the Church under changing historical circumstances, Bonhoeffer warns his readers against any facile contempt for traditional forms of the Church and against hasty attempts at structural reforms. True love for the Church will bear with great patience its many impurities and imperfections, because it is within these that the holy presence of God can be found. It is impatience as an expression of too little love that lies behind the many forms of perfectionism from the early Church (Montanism, Donatism, and so on) to the Anabaptists of the sixteenth century to the latest movements (Bonhoeffer mentions St. Simon, Tolstoy, and religious socialism) that would realize the kingdom of God here and now. Bonhoeffer's Lutheran perspective on these types of perfectionism is particularly apt when applied to the frequently spiritualistic history of Anglo-Saxon Christianity.

Another question that Bonhoeffer touches upon is whether the Church is to be understood specifically as the local congregation, while the larger groupings of Christians are simply organizations set up for utilitarian goals. Though rejecting the Catholic position that in some sense, the total Church is the sum of and also more than its local congregations, he also dissociates himself from any Congregationalist view that would give some special status in the communion of saints to the local gathering of Christians. Indeed, Bonhoeffer repudiates as dogmatically invalid the entire question concerning the smallest sociological unit of the entity Church. Such a question betrays a false understanding of the Body of Christ. Bonhoeffer, in passing here, makes the somewhat startling statement that if such a smallest unit were to be isolated at all, it would not be the local congregation but the partners in a Christian marriage!

Bonhoeffer then proceeds to discuss specific sociological functions of the empirical Church: the assembly for worship, the ministerial office, the cultic actions, and the care of souls. The assembly of Christians follows as a necessary consequence of the centrality of the Word in the Church. It is around the preached Word that the Christian congregation assembles, and this is in accordance with God's will. It goes without saying, Bonhoeffer adds, that the coming to such assemblies is not necessary to salvation. There will always be individual Christians (sick, exiled, or in other circumstances of isolation) who will be unable to attend the gathered assemblies. Nevertheless, even they exist as Christians only because at some time the Word of God reached them through the service of other Christians gathered around the proclamation of the Gospel. The Word of God is proclaimed in the historical, empirical churches: "The assembly of the faithful remains our mother." [22] Psychologically speaking, one can explain one's adherence to the visible Christian assembly only in words similar to those one would use if asked why one loves one's mother. Only such love can overcome the many social scandalizations always present in the physical congregating of

Christians, who remain what they are—Greeks, Jews, Pietists, liberals, often concrete types that may be obnoxious and irritating—and yet, in the very act of assembling under God's Word, become something else, something transfigured in Christ's presence. And the very particularities of those who sit side by side in such congregations is a reminder of God's will that we should love one another. God wills the congregating of Christians in the world. And for this purpose He uses social and psychological processes.

A very interesting and still timely part of Bonhoeffer's practical considerations is his discussion of the nuclear congregation *(Kerngemeinde)*; that is, the smaller, informal, more intensely committed gathering of Christians within the larger ecclesiastical institutions. The important difference between the two is this: the public congregation is "a part of the world organized purely out of the communion of saints." [23] By contrast, all forms of private congregations function as Christian legitimations of already existing social patterns: the natural "house church," the family, a circle of friends, and so on. The growth of private gatherings of Christians as against their public assemblies is thus to be seen as a retrogressive phenomenon, a symptom of the lack of spiritual vitality and seriousness within the Christian congregations in question.

In discussing this problem Bonhoeffer once more utilizes Luther's thoughts on similar matters. In his introduction to the *German Mass* of 1526 Luther speaks approvingly of small, informal gathering of Christians for the purpose of prayer, reading of Scripture, administration of the sacraments, and moral discipline. But Luther makes clear that such gatherings are not to be confused with the visible communion of saints, and they do not constitute a more real Church. As soon as one does that, one is in danger of forming what Luther called "hordes." This danger, Bonhoeffer feels, is always present in the concept of a nuclear congregation—the model case being the Pietist *ecclesiola in Ecclesia* (the Methodist "classes" would be comparable in the Anglo-Saxon world).

The following side remarks of Bonhoeffer are so timely to our present American situation, with its emphasis on small groups (let alone on "group dynamics") in the Church, that it is worth while to quote them in full: "There have been complaints that communion services in large city congregations suffer from the fact that the participants do not know each other. The seriousness of brotherly community is there supposed to be weakened and the celebration to lack personal warmth. Against this one may ask: Is not just such a congregation an overwhelming sermon on the significance and reality of the communion of saints going beyond any human community? Is not the witness to Christian community and brotherly love clearest in those places where it is protected against any confusion with any human communities of sympathy? Is not here the serious reality of the *sanctorum communio* to be preserved more readily—where Jew remains Jew, Greek remains Greek, worker remains worker, and capitalist remains capitalist—and yet all are the Body of Christ—than in situations where the harshness of this is mildly veiled?" [24] The real problem of such situations, according to Bonhoeffer, is not the lack of naturally given social ties, but the inadequacy of much preaching in such churches, whose ministers are only rarely "metropolitans to the metropolitans."

In this connection, Bonhoeffer enters into an elaborate argument against the typologies of "sects" and "churches" set up by Max Weber and Ernst Troeltsch. This argument is based very largely on rather gross misunderstanding of the sociological use of these typologies, but it would serve no purpose to go into these questions here. Suffice it to say that (quite rightly) Bonhoeffer maintains that these sociological concepts cannot help us in a dogmatic understanding of the Church. More interesting is his clear distinction between faith in the communion of saints and the "experience of the

Church." Here, in very practical terms, Bonhoeffer's deeply Lutheran ecclesiology becomes very clear once again.

The Christian wills the Church, belongs to the Church, finds himself in the Church as a result of his faith. But he cannot construct the Church. Any engineering thoughts concerning congregational life ("how to make a better Church," "how to vitalize the Church," and all the other "how to" questions about the life of Christian communities) are based on mistaken ecclesiologies. Nor is it necessary that the Church become an element of religious experience. One must sharply distinguish between the communion of the saints and any communitarian romanticism. It is barely conceivable that Bonhoeffer's polemic on this point was occasioned by the beginnings of Frank Buchman's Oxford Movement (aptly called Group Movement in German at this time), but, needless to say, it is equally applicable to other forms of communitarian irregularity. Against any of these forms there are very serious dogmatic reservations. The Church is an object of faith, not of emotional experience or empirical perception. As Luther said, the Church is "impalpable," "insensible." It must be believed. But the object of this faith is not an invisible Church, not the congregation of the saints as it may exist in heaven. It is faith in the presence of Christ in the empirical, historical, social reality of the world. The romantic exaltation to be found in the community of like-minded people (for example, mountain-top experiences, as fostered by the American retreat movements) mainly serves to confuse the issue. Experiences of this kind mistakenly identify human sympathies with Christian *agape*. The only protection against such confusion is extreme soberness. As Bonhoeffer concludes: "Our time is not poor in experiences but in faith. Only faith creates true experience of the Church. Therefore, we believe that it is more important to lead our time towards faith in the community of God, rather than to manufacture experiences which are useless in themselves but appear of themselves where there is faith in the *sanctorum communio*." [25]

The book concludes with a brief discussion of the relationship of ecclesiology and eschatology. As long as history lasts, we must believe rather than see. History cannot bring the solution to our problems of faith. There is no progress in history. As the German historian Ranke put it, "each epoch is immediately towards God." Church history in its entirety cannot teach us any other lesson. Christian eschatology points toward the perfection of the Church and of the entire world, not in this but in the next aeon. Only eschatologically can we believe that the objective spirit of the Church will become identical with the Holy Spirit. Then also will the experience of the Church be identical with the experience of Christ really present among His people. In other words, only then will believing have become seeing.

If we are now to sum up our comments on Bonhoeffer's *Sanctorum Communio*, we should first stress that their critical tendency is not intended to disparage casually this early work of a man whose name today can be pronounced only with the deepest respect. True respect, however, does not mean a suspension of the critical faculties. This is especially evident in view of the very young age at which this book was written. Only hagiographers will expect their subjects to be equally important on all problems and in all their utterances. We can learn so much from Bonhoeffer's later writings and even more from the profound witness of his whole life that we need not be unduly disturbed if this particular work is less than conclusive in its argument.

Nevertheless, *Sanctorum Communio* is a helpful book if only Bonhoeffer's ecclesiological position is separated from his particular philosophical and sociological presuppositions. Nor is this too difficult to do, since these presuppositions are really to be understood as foils for an essentially dogmatic argument.

If we look at Bonhoeffer's ecclesiology in isolation from its dubious prolegomena, we find here a position of astounding maturity for a young theologian just embarking on his academic career. We would not venture to decide how original this position is. But there can be no doubt that we have here a clear and at times eloquent restatement of a deeply Evangelical understanding of the Church. Especially a Lutheran doctrine of the Church will find itself enriched both by the constructive and the polemic phases of Bonhoeffer's ecclesiological argument. As we have tried to show, certain portions of the argument are particularly germane to our contemporary American church situation.

It is evident that we must confess to a much more negative evaluation of *Sanctorum Communio* in terms of the promise held out by its subtitle. We cannot recommend this work as a fruitful starting point for the much-needed dialogue between theology and the social sciences. Whatever one's concept of the social sciences might be, only those with a very particular philosophical position are likely to find Bonhoeffer's view of this relationship meaningful in any of its parts. But quite apart from Bonhoeffer's philosophical language and its difficulties for those outside this frame of reference, Bonhoeffer's choice of sociological schools carries within it the seeds of most that is unacceptable in his argument. The latter would have gained greatly (and been changed fundamentally) if in addition to the formalists it had taken into consideration the sociological approaches of Weber, Durkheim, and even Marx. In saying this, we would leave open the question whether a better understanding of Simmel would not also lead to different results.

Bonhoeffer's concepts of social reality in *Sanctorum Communio* lead to an extreme sociological realism that can with the greatest of ease become a full-blown social mythology. The reiterated use of the Hegelian concept of objective spirit shows this danger most clearly. In this way, human institutions, which exist only by virtue of human actions and human meanings, take on a strange character of independent being. Figments of our imagination come back to haunt us as demanding ghosts that squash our freedom and distort our perception of reality. Against this sort of sociological Hegelianism there is no better corrective than Weber's painful insistence on the subjective quality of all social phenomena—or Marx's insight that it is not consciousness that creates life, but life that creates consciousness. In other words, those of the American sociologist W. I. Thomas, the reality of social situations is a matter of definition—and it is always individual human beings who do the defining. There is also in Bonhoeffer's conception of science a fundamental lack of appreciation of the force of the empirical. This is understandable in a young scholar with the philosophical background of German idealism. It is likely to be severely irritating to anyone steeped in an Anglo-American tradition of empirical thought.

We would contend that there is a much livelier appreciation of social reality in Bonhoeffer's later and especially his latest works—the *Ethics* and the correspondence from prison. Here, of course, Bonhoeffer evaluated certain direct experiences of vital aspects of society, experiences brought about by his passionate engagement in men's social and political struggles. It is a pity that Bonhoeffer never returned systematically to the sociological subject matter of *Sanctorum Communio*. It might be safe to guess that his earlier argument would have had to be revised in many places.

The author of these comments has written elsewhere on the Christian implications of sociological thought and it would be pointless as well as tasteless to conclude now with a summary of his own views in the matter. Suffice it to elaborate briefly on some points emerging directly from the critical analysis of Bonhoeffer's sociological presuppositions. The following points would seem especially relevant in terms of a possible contribution of sociology to ecclesiology:

• The tendency of sociological thought, with few exceptions, is toward a nominalistic rather than a realistic understanding of social reality. Empirical perspectives on society do not allow us to construct an ontology of institutions. To speak of the family, the nation, the religious community, and so on, is permissible as an exploratory device, but only as long as we do not forget the character of institutions as humanly invented and humanly maintained conventions. It is one thing to understand the functional utility of these social fictions. It is quite another thing to posit these fictions as the essential realities of human existence. The fictitiousness (or, if one prefers, the conventionality) of social institutions is especially important to remember when we ask ourselves ethical questions. To personalize social institutions is almost inevitably the first step in the direction of an antihumanistic conception of ethics. Bonhoeffer is quite correct in asserting that only persons can be bearers of ethical value. But the consequence of this insight is *not*, as Bonhoeffer argues, that therefore certain institutions must be conceived in personal terms. It is rather that *no* institutions can be of ethical significance in and of themselves, but only insofar as they serve and protect real persons—that is, real and individual human beings. We would also contend (without thereby falling into a Christian rationalization of democratic liberalism) that this humanistic bias follows necessarily out of Christian ethics and anthropology.

• Sociology in itself is neither conservative nor radical in its political consequences. But social thought of the realistic type is peculiarly prone to becoming a conservative ideology. Crudely put, the social arrangements of a particular historical situation are given ontological status in this type of thought; and a stamp of necessity is thus impressed upon something that, at best, is a happy solution to certain problems of the moment. This process has been well analyzed in Karl Mannheim's sociology of knowledge, particularly his several studies of conservative thought.

• The sociology of religion is an empirical discipline. It is not concerned with contemplating the essence of the social reality of religious movement, but with specific empirical data concerning them. Such empirical data lead to much sharper questions addressed to theology (and especially ecclesiology) than the ones taken up by Bonhoeffer. Thus ecclesiology must come to grips with the very disturbing functionalities of religion that the sociology of religion has analyzed. Examples of this would be the integrative function of religion in both primitive and advanced societies (Durkheim), the role played by religion in providing "social theodicies" that rationalize oppression and inequality (Weber), or the relationship of religion to the irrational forces that underlie social processes (Pareto), or the relationship of religion to specific forms of false consciousness that distort our perception of society (Mannheim). We would contend that such sociological questions will immeasurably sharpen the dialectic between what is believed and what is seen in terms of our conception of the Church.

In conclusion, we would state our conviction that the main features of the ecclesiology traced in the second part of *Sanctorum Communio* would be quite capable of entering into the intellectual construction necessary to cope with these questions. In other words, Bonhoeffer's ecclesiology can serve quite well as the theological partner for the dialogue to be sought. We shall have to turn to other sources to find the sociological partner. We would contend that a Weberian sociology is likely to be the best choice for such an enterprise.

Notes for Essay 3

1 Dietrich Bonhoeffer, *Sanctorum Communio* (Munich: Chr. Kaiser Verlag, 1954). References "*S.C.*" below are to this edition.

2 John Godsey, *The Theology of Dietrich Bonhoeffer* (Philadelphia: The Westminster Press, 1960), pp. 27ff.

3 *Ibid.*, p. 21.

4 *Cf.* Horst Stephan and Martin Schmidt, *Geschichte der deutschen evangelischen Theologie* (Berlin: Toepelmann, 1960), pp. 316ff.

5 *S.C.*, pp. 11ff.

6 *Cf.* Raymond Aron, *La sociologie allemande* (Paris: Presses Universitaires, 1950), Part II.

7 *S.C.*, pp. 16ff.

8 *S.C.*, pp. 28ff.

9 *S.C.*, p. 33.

10 *Cf.* Ernst von Aster, *Geschichte der Philosophie* (Stuttgart: Kroener, 1956), pp. 367ff.

11 *S.C.*, pp. 35ff.

12 *S.C.*, p. 45.

13 *S.C.*, p. 52. Our italics. Excerpt used by permission of the publisher, Chr. Kaiser Verlag, Munich.

14 *S.C.*, pp. 64ff. The concept is taken from Hegel's *Philosophie des Geistes*, pp. 483ff.

15 *S.C.*, pp. 69f.

16 *S.C.*, p. 80.

17 *S.C.*, pp. 81ff.

18 *S.C.*, pp. 153ff.

19 *S.C.*, p. 156.

20 *S.C.*, pp. 156f.

21 *S.C.*, p. 158.

22 *S.C.*, p. 171.

23 *S.C.*, p. 173.

24 *S.C.*, p. 185.

25 *S.C.*, p. 212.

4

The Methods of Asking the Question
Concerning Jesus Christ

In his first book Bonhoeffer stood between the sociologists and the theologians; in his second, between the philosophers and the theologians. It is a significant and attractive aspect of his thought that in an age of "Either/Or" thinking, he was catholic and synthetic in wanting the best of both worlds. Like Sanctorum Communio, Act and Being belongs to his earliest academic period. Later his concern for concrete revelation led him to more concrete expression; again, the newcomer may do well to defer study of this essay until later. But again for understanding the progression and continuity of his thought this second dissertation is vital in its sequential place.

Viewed through the spectacles which Bonhoeffer's concept of nonreligious Christianity provides, and in spite of its unnecessarily turgid prose, Act and Being takes on an entirely new character and may with justice also be termed (as Barth called Bonhoeffer's first book) a theological miracle. Is it not remarkable that a twenty-five year old student should have had the acumen and intuition to take on the major methodological themes not only of the men his generation was in part to leave behind (Seeberg and others) but also to anticipate those of men centrally reckoned with today (Barth, of course; Bultmann, Heidegger, Tillich)? Has the theological world really moved much beyond the statements of those issues in three decades? More important: will it not be helped if it reaches back to Act and Being for some sense of resolution? A new English translation (Harper, 1962), will make this act possible for many students of his work.

In Act and Being Bonhoeffer first criticizes the idea of "religious a priori"—as he was to do on a full scale in his last letters. In it he comes close to his most precarious ideas of immanence when he speaks of God as being somehow "haveable, apprehensible, touchable," and material in his Church. In it he begins to attack what we might call

81

religiosity on theological and not merely psychological grounds. In it he points to God's transcendence not in a spatial beyond but in God's freedom for man in the concrete life of the Church. The sociological approach to ecclesiology in his first dissertation verges on a sociology of epistemology in the second. True, he has not yet preoccupied himself with seeing God free for man in the world so much as in the Church at this early period, but nothing he could later add would heighten the sense of the concreteness of God's revealing act wherever God chose to veil/unveil himself.

Franklin Sherman, tutor and dean of Lutheran students at Mansfield College, Oxford University and formerly of the School of Religion at the State University of Iowa, sets forth the main themes of Act and Being, regarding the book's anticipations of later work and yet sanely cautioning against seeing any intention in Bonhoeffer of developing the "nonreligious language." Dr. Sherman dealt with Bonhoeffer in his own dissertation on Christian ethics, and in a chapter for a forthcoming Meridian book on recent theologians he takes seriously the clues to Bonhoeffer presented by this early work.

Act and Being

By Franklin Sherman

"ONE Lord, one faith, one baptism"—but many theologies. This is perhaps the perennial situation of the church, but it is especially evident in an ecumenical era such as our own, when theologians of different lands and confessions can no longer indulge the luxury of ignoring one another. Is there discernible any pattern in the clash of opposing viewpoints? To what extent are theological disagreements rooted in differing philosophical presuppositions? Is not much of the problem merely semantic in character, the use of varying types of language to express what may be similar meanings? In particular, do the typically Protestant and Catholic ways of theologizing represent mutually exclusive opposites, or does each perhaps need the other as its corrective and its complement?

It was a series of questions such as these that occupied Dietrich Bonhoeffer when as a young graduate student at the University of Berlin, he prepared the postdoctoral research study that would qualify him to be appointed a lecturer in theology. The rather forbidding title of the published work (*Act and Being: Transcendental Philosophy and Ontology in Systematic Theology* [1]) is at the same time revealing of two of the writer's major conclusions: (a) that contemporary theologies are in fact groupable into two major families, which he calls theologies of act and theologies of being; and (b) that this duality can in some way be correlated with a duality in philosophical orientation. The precise nature of the correlation he discovers, we shall have to discuss further below.

Whether this treatise would ever have come to general attention except for the fame later gained by its author in other connections, is more than a little doubtful. It is written in typical academic jargon, highly complex and highly schematized. Republication of the work in German twenty-five years later and its subsequent translation into English may be attributed largely to the desire to uncover, if possible, the origins of some of the provocative ideas expressed by Bonhoeffer in his later and better-known writings. Yet the reader who has the patience to work his way through *Act and Being* will discover that it is of considerable interest in its own right. Partly this is because, of those men whom Bonhoeffer considered the leading contemporary theologians in the late 1920's, the majority are still with us in the early 1960's. Barth, Tillich, Bultmann, also the philosopher Martin Heidegger on whom Bultmann is dependent—all, by remarkable coincidence, had established the lineaments of their basic positions in the early years just preceding Bonhoeffer's study: Barth in his *Epistle to the Romans* and in the first volume of his *Dogmatics* (1927); Tillich in *The Religious Situation* (1926) and other works; Bultmann in various essays; and Heidegger in his famous *Sein und Zeit* ("Being and Time," 1927). Though in Barth's case particularly, we shall have to note changes in his later thought, for the most part Bonhoeffer's analysis of these men remains pertinent today.

What is more important is that the *problem* which Bonhoeffer isolated is still with us, whether represented by the same or different thinkers. If we consider, for example, recent discussions concerning the nature of God, Bonhoeffer's very terms *act* and *being* recur in the terminology of the two chief positions, at least as articulated on the American scene. For the one, God is the God who acts; for the other, he is the ground of being. On the one hand, we have biblical theology;

on the other hand, philosophical theology, especially as expounded by Paul Tillich. No less a person than Tillich's long-time colleague Reinhold Niebuhr has criticized Tillich's ontological speculation, his impersonal categories such as being-itself and the New Being, as inadequate to convey the biblical conception of life as a divine-human drama whose meaning is revealed in specific historical events, that is, in God's mighty acts. Theology, states Niebuhr, requires language appropriate to that to which it witnesses. "It may be," he suggests, "that selves, wills, the sins of selves and the grace of the love by which selves are saved from sin—that all these realities can be stated only in dramatic-poetic form," which means in our present context: in act-categories. But Tillich replies that a theology which, by definition, deals with ultimacy, cannot avoid asking about the standing of all such terms and entities "within the whole of being." [2]

The same set of alternatives appears in connection with other issues. Discussion of the nature of the church, at least in certain continental circles, has turned on the question of whether the church is to be understood as event or institution. Is the church an ever-repeated happening, actualized in the moment of response to the Gospel, or is it an organized structure with continuity in time and space? On the topic of the Holy Communion, even those who agree on the real presence of Christ in the sacrament disagree on whether that presence is attached, so to speak, to the action of the sacrament, or is in some way a substantial presence localized in the elements. And how is grace itself to be conceived? Only as God's personal favor (act), or also as a quasi-physical entity that can be infused into the soul (being)? With respect to Christology, voices have been heard calling for a functional Christology, an interpretation of the significance of Jesus Christ in terms of what he accomplished for man's salvation (his redemptive deeds, his mighty acts) rather than a static conception of two natures. And in the whole Catholic-Protestant discussion, whether between Roman Catholicism and Protestantism in the denominational sense, or between Catholic and Protestant elements within a communion such as Anglicanism, Protestants are commonly accused of impoverishing theology by their inability or unwillingness to think ontologically, that is, in "being" categories; and the Catholics in turn are charged by the Protestants with distorting the faith by their very use of such categories.[3]

Bonhoeffer disclaims any intention of providing a fully detailed and balanced analysis of all the thinkers that he deals with; his interest, he avers, is not historical but systematic. That is to say, he admits that he may ignore certain qualifying elements in the teaching of a given thinker, in order to use him more readily as an example of a certain type of thought. To use Bonhoeffer's own term, his interpretation is stylized. This proviso, however, is probably meant to apply primarily to his discussion of the philosophical background of modern theology. When he comes to deal with the contemporary theologians themselves, it is fairly clear that he wishes his criticisms of Barth, Tillich, Gogarten, Holl, and others to be applied in a literal sense, which would be meaningless if his exposition of their thought could not be taken as historically accurate, or at least as so intended by the author.

It seems clear, too, that the impetus for Bonhoeffer's investigation was derived from a particular historical development—namely, from the constantly increasing influence of Karl Barth's theology in the Germany of the 1920's. The young theologian at Berlin felt the necessity of coming to terms with this prophetic figure who had so unsettled the assumptions of prewar religiousness. Later, the two were to make common cause in the church struggle against Nazism, Bonhoeffer acknowledging Barth as the ideological leader of the struggle. The former's own thinking and writing during the 1930's, moreover, was to bear a strongly Barthian imprint. As Barth had proclaimed the transcendence of God, the Kierkegaardian "infinite qualitative difference" between God and man, so Bonhoeffer was to interpret the Christian life in *The Cost of Discipleship* as a "radical breach with the immediacies of the world." Barth had recalled the church to a theology of the Word, founded on exegesis; it was to biblical studies rather than systematic theology that Bonhoeffer was to turn his energies. Barth had decried all natural theology, and was to do so even more emphatically. Bonhoeffer joined him in this denial, contending especially against what appeared to be the social-ethical equivalent of natural theology, the Lutheran doctrine of orders of creation. In many respects, then, the young Bonhoeffer might justly have been regarded as one of Karl Barth's disciples, at least as viewed from the perspective of the very different sort of theology then prevailing in the Anglo-Saxon world. It is significant that during the year Bonhoeffer spent at Union Theological Seminary in New York immediately following the completion of *Act and Being* (1930–1931), he chose to devote one of his major seminar papers to the explication and defense of Barth's theology. The paper has been preserved, and we can note in it Bonhoeffer's assertion that with Barth "we stand in the tradition of Paul, Luther, Kierkegaard, in the tradition of genuine Christian thinking." The theology of crisis, he states, amounts simply to an effort to take with absolute seriousness once again the biblical and Reformation doctrine of justification by faith.[4] We may be sure, then, that whatever criticisms of Barth we find in *Act and Being* were made from within a profound sympathy with his aims and achievements.

How shall God's revelation be interpreted? This is the central question in Bonhoeffer's study. That he can assume that Christian theology as well as Christian faith itself is dependent on revelation, is a tribute to the effectiveness of Barth's Copernican revolution against a theology that had founded itself rather on religious experience. Bonhoeffer appears to have been powerfully influenced also by Luther's

Commentary on Romans, with its insistence that our salvation depends on a righteousness "which does not originate in ourselves but comes to us from beyond ourselves," to which indeed our experience may be quite contradictory.[5] Man's proper stance before God is in the first instance passive rather than active, receptive rather than productive. Yet if revelation does come to us from beyond ourselves, it is nevertheless to us that it comes, and our thinking about it, therefore, is inevitably formulated in human terms and categories. On this truth Bonhoeffer is equally insistent. Implied here is that theology cannot consist merely in the repetition of biblical words and phrases, even if preaching could. Bonhoeffer presupposes that revelation is meant to be understood; but to understand means to bring within some universe of discourse. Even a theology of the Word of God cannot avoid using the words of men.

It is for this reason that the theologian cannot avoid all intercourse with the philosopher, since the latter's special vocation (according to one major school of thought at least) is precisely the clarification of words, concepts, and relations between universes of discourse. Bonhoeffer's concern is that the theologian's utilization of philosophy should not remain at the level of unconscious influence, but should be a self-conscious and, even more important, a critical utilization. His question to Barth is whether the latter has in fact been sufficiently critical with regard to the influence of Kantian philosophy upon his thought.

The greatness of Kant, as Bonhoeffer points out in the present work and as Barth would agree,[6] lies in the clarity with which he perceived the limits of human reason. The component parts of the process by which man has gained whatever knowledge he does possess, Kant analyzed with marvelous thoroughness. But at the same time, he cast doubts upon the scope and reliability of that knowledge. Even in the world of ordinary experience, what we take to be realities are only phenomena, appearances, according to Kant. The noumena, the things in themselves, remain beyond our grasp. Far more is this true of the so-called ultimate realities about which metaphysicians have argued. The concept of God, like that of the soul, is for Kant purely a limiting concept, serving to indicate the boundaries of our knowing. Since God by definition transcends all that is human, he can never become the object of man's knowledge; he remains in his own subjectivity. Even his existence can only be postulated, not proved.

The upshot of the matter from the standpoint of this transcendental philosophy is that I know a great deal about my act of knowing, but not so much about what is known. It is this stress on the act of knowing, apparently, that causes Bonhoeffer to characterize Kant's as an "act" philosophy √ rather than a philosophy of being. Involved here is the special meaning which the term act had assumed in German thought, largely under the influence of the late nineteenth-century philosopher and psychologist Franz Brentano. He had maintained that it is "the mental act (for example, the act of sensing a red color patch) rather than the content itself (for example, the red color)" that is the proper subject matter of psychology.[7] The philosopher Edmund Husserl (1859–1938), whom Bonhoeffer exposits at some length, had developed this point in his notion of intentionality, the property of the human mind by virtue of which it "intends" or refers to an object that presumably lies outside of it. Whether this object really exists is another question. As Bonhoeffer summarizes this phenomenological viewpoint: "To be sure, every act intends an object, consciousness is always 'awareness of x,' but whether this 'intentional object' envisaged by consciousness is also a real object is irrelevant. . . ."[8]

It is this trend of thought which Bonhoeffer sees as having influenced Karl Barth's theology. Not, of course, that Barth denies the existence of God in the common-sense meaning of that word; but he does deny that God exists in the realm of objectivity. God is not graspable by our thought, not even by that kind of thought called theology. At the most, God can use a theology to witness to himself. He is not bound even by the word of Scripture, if considered as an objectively given entity. We know him only when and where he today chooses to reveal himself. A passage quoted by Bonhoeffer from Barth's *Christian Dogmatics* of 1927 epitomizes this viewpoint:

> Now it would follow that the relationship between God and man in which God's revelation may truly be imparted to me, a man, must be a free, not a static relationship, in the sense that its very constancy can never mean anything other than constancy in a transaction not simply continuous, but at every moment beginning, in all seriousness, at the beginning. It may never be conceived as already given, already obtaining, or even as analogous to a natural law or a mathematical function. Rather, one must always think of it as "act-ual" (*aktuell*), that is, with all the instability of a deed in the course of execution.[9]

Bonhoeffer acknowledges the greatness of this sort of statement as a testimony to God's sovereign freedom. Nevertheless he has a number of questions to put to it. The first and most fundamental concerns the nature of God's freedom. Is the freedom to speak or not to speak, the freedom to give or to withhold himself from man, really the freedom of the God we know in Christ? Has not Barth fallen into the error of dealing with possibilities—with what God can or cannot do, might or might not do—rather than cleaving to the reality in which God has in fact revealed himself? As Bonhoeffer declares, in one of his most remarkable passages:

> In revelation it is not so much a question of God's freedom beyond it, i.e., his eternal isolation and aseity, but rather of God's coming forth, his coming out of himself in the revelation, of his given Word, of his covenant in which he has bound himself—of his freedom which

finds its strongest attestation precisely in his having freely bound himself to historical man, in his placing himself at man's disposal. *God is not free from man, but for man.* Christ is the Word of the freedom of God. God is "there," which is to say: not in eternal non-objectivity, but—let us say it with all due caution—"haveable," graspable in his Word within the church.[10]

Bonhoeffer thus propounds what he terms a material as contrasted with Barth's formal understanding of God's freedom; or, as we may put it in the present context, a *concrete* as over against an abstract understanding of it.

The second question is related to the first, and concerns the nature of the limits to man that are set by God's transcendence. Kantian philosophy, as we have noted, stresses the limits to man's rational capacities. But does this constitute a genuine limit? If human reason by its cleverness has discerned its own limits, has it not by this very fact become lord over these limits? As Bonhoeffer points out (applying an insight of Hegel), a limit can be understood only by a mind that has in some sense passed beyond it, and can view it from both sides, as it were. "Essentially," he writes, "reason *has no* bounds, for in principle the very bound can be thought away until it is no more a genuine boundary." [11] Thus an epistemological conception of man's limitations is self-defeating. Yet it is with this side of the question, Bonhoeffer implies, that the Barthian theology has been preoccupied. The biblical conception, he asserts, is quite different. Not man's reason but man's total life is limited by God's revelation. "There are bounds only to concrete man as a whole, and their name is Christ." [12]

To put the same point in other words: if man is essentially not mind but person, then he can be limited only in his encounter with God as person, that is, with Christ. And only thus does his life gain genuine meaning, for only by this encounter is he liberated from the boundlessness of his own selfhood. Boundlessness is meaninglessness: only the limit gives life real definition. Thus, though the limit is judgment, it also is grace.

But how can I encounter God as person in Christ? The phrase as it stands is still too abstract for Bonhoeffer. With the aid of a concept developed in his doctoral dissertation *Sanctorum Communio* (and utilized later also in his lectures on Christology), he presses the notion of encounter with God to its ultimate point of concreteness. I meet God in Christ; but I meet Christ in the church, for the church *is* the contemporary Christ—it is "Christ existing as community" *(Christus als Gemeinde existierend).*

Thus it is in meeting my neighbor, that is, in encountering him as person within the personal community of the church, that I encounter my limit in its most tangible form. The undeniable objectivity of the other man, both in his claims and in his gifts, at last convinces me that the meaning of my life does not arise from within me, but comes to me from outside of me. This is what Bonhoeffer had already identified in his previous dissertation as an ethical rather than epistemological idea of transcendence. He acknowledges his indebtedness at this point to the philosopher Eberhard Grisebach (whose viewpoint in turn is closely comparable to that of Martin Buber's *I and Thou).* But Grisebach, he observes, underestimates the power of the human ego to pull even the claim of the neighbor into the maelstrom of its own egocentric absolutism, unless that claim be sustained by the presence within it of the divine Thou. For Bonhoeffer, it is not my neighbor as such, but Christ in my neighbor, who is the authentic limit to my life.

The third question that Bonhoeffer puts to actualistic theology concerns the reality and continuity of the life of faith. Is my own faith as elusive and nonobjective as the concept of God is from this standpoint? Does faith not have any existence apart from the moment in which God chooses to reveal himself, so that, as Barth says, it begins again and again at the beginning? But what then could Paul have meant by speaking of the life "in" Christ, or by admonishing Christians to stand fast "in" the Lord? Does not this imply continuity, and therefore demand some sort of "being" categories? This is a question directed by Bonhoeffer not only at Barth but also at Bultmann. According to the latter's doctrine of man, founded as it is on his existentialist presuppositions, life itself consists in decision. Man's career is not to be understood as process, but as event; not as nature, but as history. The Gospel is a message that puts me inescapably under the necessity of decision, and at the same time gives me the possibility of deciding for Christ, that is, for "authentic" existence (Heidegger). But if existence is decision, how then, asks Bonhoeffer, can its continuity be envisaged? "The question is: how and with what right are we to think of existence, in particular the new existence, as a unified whole? . . . Is being in Christ constituted only by every conscious act of decision for Christ?" [13]

The answer to this question, as to the previous one concerning man's concrete limits, can be found, Bonhoeffer declares, only by taking the church seriously. Before developing this answer in his own terms, however, he first considers the various theologies of being. Common to these viewpoints is the note of objectivity rather than subjectivity, the conviction that "being precedes consciousness" rather than vice versa. Here we have the influence not of transcendental philosophy but of ontology; not of a theory of knowledge but of a theory of being. The very term "onto-logy," as Bonhoeffer remarks, contains in its Greek roots "the clash of two mighty claims," those of being (Greek ōn) and thought (logos—word, discourse, reason). Genuine ontology rests on the conviction that logos must surrender its claim to supremacy. Thought does not produce being, but reflects it. Indeed, insofar as thought "is," it is an aspect of being, like everything that is.

But if thought thus plays the dependent role, the very fact

that it believes itself to be determined by being gives it a confidence that it is accurately reflecting the latter. Theologies influenced by ontological philosophy will thus have a much greater assurance than act-theologies about the adequacy of their own statements about God, man, faith, revelation, and the like. They will think of revelation not as God's momentary self-disclosure, but in some sense as an objectively given entity which man can rely upon. Professor Ernst Wolf, in his introduction to the reprint of Bonhoeffer's book, sums up the contrast somewhat more clearly than the author himself had done. As he puts it, Bonhoeffer had traced the opposing "theological fronts" in the German theology of the time back to "the encounter of a theology of 'act' (contingency, discontinuity, transcendentalism, reference to existence, and decision) with a theology of 'being' (givenness, continuity, metaphysics, objectification, and 'doctrine')." [14]

Bonhoeffer describes three forms of being-theology, varying as to the nature of the "given entity" with which they identify revelation. The first identifies revelation with doctrine; the second, with psychic experience; the third, with a divinely established institution. The common failing of all three, according to Bonhoeffer's argument, is that they place revelation at man's disposal—not paradoxically, as in the author's own view indicated above, but directly. Thereby they lose the true character of revelation, which must, by definition, strike man from without, at its own free initiative.

If revelation is understood as doctrine, the problem of continuity is solved. Doctrine is always there, always accessible. But doctrine as such cannot touch and transform man's existence. As Bonhoeffer writes, in a passage that anticipates his polemic against "cheap grace" in *The Cost of Discipleship*,

> Even a doctrine of the merciful God, even one which states that wherever man and God come together, there the Cross must stand—even such a doctrine is no stum-

bling block (at least to our modern way of thinking), but rather a wholly welcome addition to our "system." The stumbling block, the scandal, arises only when our existence is really affected, when we not only hear of the Cross and judgment but, hearing, must needs deliver ourselves to them, that grace may descend.[15]

As to the interpretation of revelation as religious experience, this has already been referred to as a position vanquished by the Barthian theology, and Bonhoeffer mentions it only briefly in the present connection. The third being-interpretation is "revelation as institution." This he sees expressed in two forms: the Roman Catholic concept of the church, and Protestant orthodoxy's concept of the verbally inspired Bible. In both cases, revelation is eminently objectified and available. The verbal-inspiration theory Bonhoeffer also passes by with only a few comments; he plainly does not consider it a live option today any more than the theology of religious experience.

Roman Catholicism with its stress on the church as the locus and embodiment of revelation is definitely "on the right track," in Bonhoeffer's view. If the Catholic position, as he interprets it, amounts to the assertion that "whoever is in the institution is in God," this does not sound very different from Bonhoeffer's own assertion quoted above.[16] But there are two crucial differences. In the first place, Bonhoeffer does not think of the church as a hierarchical institution, but as a personal community. "The being of an institution," he writes, "is incapable of affecting the existence of man as sinful; it cannot stand over against him, be ob-jective (gegen-ständlich) in the full sense. That is only possible in the real meeting with another person." [17] And, second, Bonhoeffer emphasizes far more than does Roman Catholicism the church's dependence on the preached Word. These two points coalesce, for they are both corollaries of his conviction that the church's being is constituted by Christ himself. Christ is the subject of the proclamation, and he is the subject of the congregation. Or, as Bonhoeffer can say with the use of another concept from his *Sanctorum Communio*, Christ is the corporate person of the Christian community. "It is here that Christ has come the very nearest to humanity, here given himself to his new humanity, so that his person enfolds in itself all whom he has won." [18]

The church as personal community is the unity of act and being. It is act in that it exists only by virtue of the act of faith, understood as genuine faith in God, and not faith in faith. Bonhoeffer distinguishes between a direct act of faith, which looks wholly outside of itself, and a reflexive act which looks back on itself; only the former really grasps revelation. This faith, however, is not only my personal faith, but the faith of the church, which as the believing community has being, has continuity in time and space. This believing community is prior to my own life as believer, since it already exists when I am born into it by baptism. Infant baptism is prized by Bonhoeffer precisely because it expresses this priority, this givenness of the church. We have then the paradox that the being of revelation, namely, the church, exists only in faith; yet only that faith is genuine which acknowledges that revelation does not *depend* on faith. These two propositions, Bonhoeffer declares, "must combine to make a third: only in faith does man know that the being of revelation, his own being in the church, is independent of faith." [19] Or, as he also summarizes the matter: the conflict between the subjectivism of act-theology and the false externalization of being-theologies is overcome by the use of a theosociological category. "The being of revelation, as hovering between the objective and the non-objective, is 'person'—the revealed person of God and the personal community of which that person is the foundation." [20]

In addition to these criticisms regarding the nature of the church, Bonhoeffer has one further objection to Roman Catholic thought as an example of being-theology. This is its assumption that *neutral* ontological categories are possible and desirable as the foundation of Christian theology. Human reason as such, according to Roman Catholicism (which means according to St. Thomas Aquinas) is capable of discerning truths about the being of both God and man which, though they do require supplementation from revelation, are reliable as far as they go. These two types of truth are most closely related, truth-about-God being based on and projected from truth-about-man (and the rest of creation). As one Roman Catholic authority (not quoted by Bonhoeffer) states: "Inasmuch as our minds, in common with the natural objects of our experience, are made according to the exemplar of the Divine Mind, the knowledge gained from God's material and spiritual creations brings us valid, though partial, understanding of their primary Cause." [21]

This type of theology, in other words, assumes that a doctrine of creation (of God as Creator and of man as creature) is derivable quite apart from revelation. But to think thus, says Bonhoeffer, is to think abstractly. Man does not exist apart from revelation: he exists in relation to revelation, whether that relation be one of judgment or grace. In the concrete, man is never merely creature; he is either sinner or saved. What we have to ask of the Thomist theory, Bonhoeffer writes, is "whether there is in fact a being of man which is not already determined as his 'being in Adam' or 'being in Christ,' as his being-guilty or being-blessed-with-grace." [22] Statements about the being of God apart from his relation to man are equally dubious. "Primarily," Bonhoeffer asserts, "God is not the sheer Is: he 'is' the just one, 'is' the holy one, he 'is' love. Theological concepts of being must have precisely this as their ontological premise, that the Is can in no way be detached from the concrete definition." [23]

"Being in Adam" and "being in Christ"—these are the categories with which Bonhoeffer counters the attempted neutralism of Thomistic as well as other types of ontology (Husserl, Scheler, and Heidegger are also discussed). At the same time, these categories serve to counter the occasionalism of pure act-theology. With respect to the nature of sin, for example, Bonhoeffer acknowledges that this must be understood as act, specifically as the act of the human will, which as a will "curved in on itself" seeks itself rather than God. Yet sin is also a state in which we find ourselves. "If sin were no more than the occasional free act, it would be possible to find one's way back to a sinless being; revelation in Christ would have become redundant." [24] The term "being in Adam" is perfectly suited, Bonhoeffer suggests, to express this duality of sin as act and as state of being, since Adam, in accordance with its Hebrew meaning, can refer both to the individual man and to the corporate, sinful humanity in the midst of which every man finds himself. There is no such thing as an isolated individual, Bonhoeffer declares. "I am I and humanity in one."

> In my fall from God, humanity fell. And so the I's debt before the Cross grows to monstrous dimensions; it is the very Adam, the very first to do the inconceivable deed, which it does again and again: sin as act. But in this act, whose whole burden I continue to lay on myself with each sinful occasion, I find myself already in the humanity of Adam; I see that in me, necessarily, humanity does this my own free deed.[25]

Likewise the new life in Christ, that is, in the church, is at the same time act and being. I am the bearer of the new humanity, yet I am also borne by it. This is the dialectic between faith and church.

> In reality I hear another man declare the Gospel to me, see him offer me the sacrament: "thou art forgiven," see and hear him and the congregation praying for me; at the same time I hear the Gospel, I join in the prayer and I know myself joined into the Word, sacrament and prayer of the congregation, the new humanity, whether this be here at the moment or elsewhere: borne by her, bearing her.[26]

It is on the basis of this new life in Christ that a doctrine of creation, which was impossible to unaided reason, may now be articulated, for in Christ man's true creaturehood is restored. In Adam, that is, in sin, proud man fancies himself the creator. Only in Christ, namely, in faith, does he truly acknowledge his creaturehood not merely as an idea but in reality. He becomes what he should have been, but never was. This is what Bonhoeffer calls "the eschatological possibility of the child." Or, as he can also put it: in Christ man's "being-there" (*Dasein*, a term borrowed from Heidegger) is released from the distortion of his "being-thus (*Wiesein*). His "that-ness" is released from the spell of his "howness," which means concretely, his sin. On the basis of the revelation in Christ, a true ontology becomes possible. This is Bonhoeffer's program for a "Christian philosophy," a philosophy that explicitly recognizes the authority of revelation. Such a program would involve, as he says, a theological rethinking of such creaturely categories as individuality, nature, and history, being and becoming, and the like. It would be an exercise in what he calls "thinking *from* the truth" rather than toward it.[27] To this we should add only that Bonhoeffer realizes that even the believer lives always "in Adam" as well as "in Christ" (this is his version of Luther's *simul justus et peccator*); such efforts at Christian philosophizing will therefore doubtless remain fragmentary.

If we review what Bonhoeffer has said in the present treatise about the relations of philosophy and theology, we find that he has developed a dialectical position. An influence of philosophy on theology is inevitable, if for no other reason than that as has been intimated, it is the philosopher whose calling it is to explore and define those concepts basic to all human discourse—concepts which theology, as a form of such discourse, cannot avoid.[28] Bonhoeffer's exposition of the philosophical influences even on Barth's theology is powerful evidence for this. But theology need not and dare not let such influences go unexamined. Its use of philosophical categories must be a self-conscious and critical one, so much so that the categories themselves are transformed. Thereby in turn, something of the import of theology for the whole range of philosophical, that is, "creaturely," questions will be discerned.

In Bonhoeffer's brief references to Tillich, the question raised is whether the latter has sufficiently appreciated the dialectical character of this relationship, especially the unsettling effect on philosophy of the concept of revelation. The same question is put to Bultmann in view of his close dependence on a particular ontology—namely, Heidegger's analysis of existence. As to Heidegger himself, Bonhoeffer evidences great appreciation for his *Sein und Zeit* and, as we have noted, adopts from it the notion of *Dasein*.[29] By interpreting being in terms of historicity, Heidegger in fact "has succeeded in forcing act and being into partnership."[31] His failure is that he has interpreted man's temporality or finitude as a self-enclosed finitude. He has left no room for revelation, or for the knowledge granted in revelation "that finiteness is creatureliness, that is, is open to God."[32] But such a failure, adds Bonhoeffer, is inevitable for any attempt at an autonomous philosophy; thought is as little able as good works to deliver man from his *cor curvum in se*, his "heart curved in on itself" (Luther).

In all that has been said in the foregoing pages about the nature of theology, it should be understood that we have been referring to theology as a distinctly intellectual enterprise within the church. As such, it is clearly distinguished by Bonhoeffer from the life of faith, on the one hand, and from the task of preaching, on the other. In a valuable section entitled "The Problem of Knowledge and the Idea of the Church," he lists three ways of knowing which correspond, he says, to three sociologically distinct functions of the church. The first is knowing as a believer. This kind of knowledge, which pertains to every Christian, is wholly existential in character. It means "knowing oneself overcome and blessed with grace by the person of Christ through the preached word." [33] The second and third types of knowledge, in contrast, are churchly in character. The preacher, says Bonhoeffer, does not speak as an individual but on behalf of the community. For himself, the preacher may well cry, "Lord, I believe, help thou mine unbelief." But when he stands in his pulpit, he no longer utters the second half of that cry.

> The preacher, as preacher for the community, must know what he preaches: Jesus Christ the crucified (I Corinthians 2:2). He has the full power to proclaim the Gospel to the hearer, to forgive sins in preaching and sacrament. There may be no uncertainty here, no not-knowing: all must be made plain from the given Word of God, who has bound himself to his revelation; for in preaching which creates faith, Christ himself deigns to preach as the subject of the spoken words. I preach, but I preach in the strength of Christ, in the strength of the community's faith, not the strength of my faith.[34]

Yet not even the preacher, Bonhoeffer adds, can escape from the necessity of reflecting on the content of his address. And thereby arises the necessity of theology, which may be simply defined as "reflective thought in the service of the church." [35] Or, as Bonhoeffer also puts it: the church cannot exist without preaching; but preaching cannot exist without remembrance; and "theology is the memory of the church." [36] The object of its reflection is all that has happened, and that has been stored up in the Bible, in the liturgy, in church history—and that is actualized again and again by preaching. Theology thus "stands between past and future preaching," aiming to gather up the meaning of the past and make it available as the foundation for the future.

This is the justification for theology; but it is not a justification for any particular theology. The theologian's work can only proceed in fear and trembling. It is a more lonely work than that of the preacher, for, as Bonhoeffer points out, their sociological positions within the church are different. The preacher is primarily in the community, and only secondarily an individual, but the theologian is primarily an individual and secondarily in the community (the believer as such being the two equally). The work of the theologian thus inevitably reflects his own limitations as an individual, not to speak of the limitations of human thought itself. And so, Bonhoeffer concludes regarding his own book, "likewise the concrete doctrine of self-understanding in revelation which is unfolded in these pages is in itself mere 'doctrine,' system, autonomous self-understanding." [37] The theologian can only offer the fruit of his thinking to the church, asking the community to assign it its place, to bestow its meaning upon it. His appropriate motto, Bonhoeffer suggests, making an adaptation of Luther's dictum, would be "Reflect bravely, but believe and rejoice in Christ more bravely still." [38]

We have by no means followed all the intricacies of Bonhoeffer's argument in *Act and Being*, and have omitted entirely some elements, for example, his critique of his own teacher Reinhold Seeberg's position on the problem.[39] But we are perhaps now in a better position to understand what the young theologian meant when he announced in the introduction to his treatise that his aim was "to unify the aims of true transcendentalism and true ontology in a 'churchly thinking.' " [40]

As to Bonhoeffer's own doctrine of the church as set forth in this work, the reader may well have reservations, especially as regards the concept of Christ as the corporate person of the church. Here Bonhoeffer seems unduly dependent on a particular sociological notion (he acknowledges the philosopher-sociologist Max Scheler as its source). His intention, however, was only to propose this as a modern equivalent for Paul's speaking of the church as the Body of Christ. It is not adequate, as he himself admits, for expressing the complementary truth of Christ's Lordship over the body, his transcendence of the church.[41]

If we do nevertheless accept the general trend of the book's argument, the question with which it leaves us is an acutely practical one: how can the church be in reality what it is in Bonhoeffer's theory? In commenting at one point on Hegel, who also attempted to reconcile all sorts of divergent emphases, Bonhoeffer remarks that Hegel forgot only to consider the reality of the concrete individual, including the philosopher, in whom all these contradictions may not at all be reconciled (this of course simply repeats Kierkegaard's basic criticism). "Hegel wrote a philosophy of angels, but not of human existence." [42] The same point might well be raised regarding the church as pictured in Bonhoeffer's dissertation—the church as the unity of act and being; the church as the genuine community where one experiences real meeting with another person; the church which is, to quote one of Bonhoeffer's most pregnant phrases, "the place where existence is understood." Where does this church itself exist? Only in God's intention, which would mean in man's future, or also in present reality?

It seems that Bonhoeffer himself was troubled with such questions; and, if there is anything that can excuse the abstractness of *Act and Being*, it is the fact that the author, in the years following its writing, threw himself into practical work designed to realize in some measure the vision of the church he had evolved in his academic treatises. Even while serving as lecturer at the university, he undertook to teach a confirmation class in a depressed area of Berlin, and subsequently founded a settlement house there. Later he gave up academic work entirely in favor of the pastorate. But the greatest expression of Bonhoeffer's concern for the concrete embodiment of his ecclesiology came in his years as director of the Confessing Church seminary at Finkenwalde, the experience which resulted in the book *Life Together*. Here we see spelled out in its significance for the daily round the complete openness to the Word of God together with openness to one another, the utter dependence on the Word and on the brother, that constituted Bonhoeffer's conception of the church. True, he is describing the life of a rather select community, that of a group of seminary students; but it is clear that he believes this kind of life to be possible also in ordinary congregations, although perhaps under other forms. If the church in its fullness does exist only in God's future, this is a future that constantly presses to incarnate itself in the present, and that calls for our faithful response in allowing the empirical church to be transformed into the real church. Life Together is, as it were, the practical handbook to Act and Being.

Partly because of his interest in new forms of communal living, Bonhoeffer was accused during the 1930's of catholicizing tendencies. We may deduce from his argument in Act and Being that he would regard this as a compliment, at least if it meant a serious concern for the continuity of Christian existence, for the concreteness of the church, and for a doctrine of grace that affirms that God really gives himself to his creatures. On the other hand, we have noted that Bonhoeffer's doctrine of grace is not at all hierarchical or institutional but personal, and furthermore that he insists on the centrality of justification by faith. In the face of catholicizing tendencies within Protestantism at the present time, therefore—whether these pertain to liturgy, the sacraments, the role of the ministry and the episcopacy, or any other such issues—it would seem that from Bonhoeffer's standpoint a twofold attitude is indicated. Insofar as they represent an acknowledgment of the being of revelation, its transsubjective reality, continuity, and concreteness, such tendencies are to be affirmed. Insofar as they reflect a search for a merely human security or authority, they are to be challenged. Revelation for Bonhoeffer is "haveable," but never manipulable.

What of his lengthy critique of Karl Barth? In this case,

Bonhoeffer was aiming at a moving target. The Barth of today is by no means the same as the Barth of thirty-five years ago. What is striking is that the *direction* in which Barth has moved is in many respects the direction toward which Bonhoeffer's early treatises pointed. This was seen already in 1932 when Barth republished the first volume of his "Christian Dogmatics" as "*Church* Dogmatics." In his ethics, Barth has shown increasing appreciation for the "constancy and continuity of the divine command," which demands a continuity in man's response as well; ethics is not to be resolved into a mere series of discrete acts or situations.[43] Most remarkable of all has been Barth's shift from his earlier exclusive emphasis on God's transcendence (which Bonhoeffer criticized as depending on an abstract notion of God's freedom), to a radical stress on God's immanence—though, to be sure, as Barth would say, it is *God's* immanence, and must be interpreted christologically. To put it otherwise, Barth appears largely to have accepted Bonhoeffer's Lutheran principle of *finitum capax infiniti* (the finite can contain the infinite) over against the Calvinistic *non capax*. His 1956 lecture on "The Humanity of God" provides the most vivid documentation of the "change of direction" (Barth's own phrase), and includes whole passages such as the following that might have been written by Bonhoeffer:

> God's deity is thus no prison in which He can exist only in and for Himself. It is rather His freedom to be in and for Himself but also with and for us, to assert but also to sacrifice Himself, to be wholly exalted but also completely humble, not only almighty but also almighty mercy, not only Lord but also servant, not only judge but also Himself the judged, not only man's eternal king but also his brother in time.[44]

Barth's doctrine of the church, however, still leaves something to be desired from the standpoint of Bonhoeffer's concern for act-being unity. In an essay prepared for the Amsterdam Assembly of the World Council of Churches, for example, Barth speaks in wholly actualistic terms: the church is the event in which two or three are gathered together in the name of Christ.[45] Barth's rejection of infant baptism is also highly significant, as is his preference for a purely congregational church order. Roman Catholic observers have commented that Barth's theology seems soundest on the great basic themes of creation, incarnation, redemption, while he is weakest on the dependent themes of the church, the sacraments, and the Christian life.[46] Perhaps it is in the latter realm that Bonhoeffer is most valuable as a supplement to Barth.

On the relation between theology and philosophy, Barth appears to have made a double movement, again bringing him out fairly close to Bonhoeffer's position. In the 1932 *Dogmatics* he admitted the philosophical biases of his earlier work, but stated that he had gone over the same and cut out from it every reference that "might give the slightest appearance" of giving theology a basis or support in philosophy. His was to be a strictly Protestant, that is, nonphilosophical, theology, "self-nourished at its own source." [47] Was this the turn that caused Bonhoeffer in his prison letters to criticize Barth's theology as a "positivism of revelation"? At any rate, the later Barth seems more ready to acknowledge that it is impossible wholly to escape from philosophical biases. In a 1953 essay, he writes: "A free theologian does not deny, nor is he ashamed of, his indebtedness to a particular philosophy or ontology, to ways of thought and speech. . . . No one speaks exclusively in Biblical terms." The theologian, however, Barth adds, must stand ready "to submit the coherence of his concepts and formulations to the coherence of the divine revelation. . . . His ontology will be subject to criticism and control by his theology, and not conversely." [48]

It is doubtful whether Bonhoeffer fully understood Tillich's intentions on this point, at least as we can now understand

them in the light of his later work. Tillich's view of the relations between philosophy and theology would appear to be
much more dialectical than Bonhoeffer thought—certainly his
Systematic Theology evidences an intricate interplay between
the two disciplines. Even if Tillich does reject the term "Christian philosophy," his own work might well be considered an
excellent example of what Bonhoeffer meant by a "theological
re-thinking of creaturely categories." On the basic issue of
combining act and being emphases, too, Bonhoeffer's views
find a close parallel in Tillich's program for maintaining or
restoring the "Catholic substance" of Christianity while not
giving up the "Protestant principle" which holds even the
church under God's judgment. "Justification by faith" and
"the New Being in Christ": for Tillich as for Bonhoeffer, these
are two sides of the same coin.[49]

In the debate between Tillich and Reinhold Niebuhr, it
seems clear that Bonhoeffer would agree with the former on
the inescapability of philosophical categories, although he
would share, too, the latter's concern lest the uniqueness of
revelation be compromised. It is evident that the conception
of act as employed by Bonhoeffer in *Act and Being* is not precisely the same as that used by Niebuhr and others in speaking
of God's mighty acts. The concepts are similar enough, however, to give a continuing pertinence to Bonhoeffer's query as
to whether such terminology can do justice to the concreteness of revelation. If Bonhoeffer's argument were taken seriously, it might at least help to allay some of the current suspicion in Protestant circles of ontological thinking, "substance"
concepts of grace, and so on. It might convince those who set
out to articulate a purely biblical theology, abjuring all "Greek
speculation," that they are not thereby released from all philosophical problems.

Whether we find in *Act and Being* any intimations of Bonhoeffer's later proposal for a "nonreligious interpretation of
theological concepts" is doubtful. His concern here is more

nearly the opposite—to make a theological interpretation of nontheological concepts. Yet a basic principle is thereby established which underlies also his later idea, a principle which we may call that of the *complementarity of languages*. This implies that no one language is adequate for the whole existence of the Christian and the church. The language of prayer is not the same as the language of theology, nor need the language of apologetics be the same as that of edification. Neither the language of act nor that of being is in itself sufficient to interpret revelation: each needs the other as its complement and corrective. Perhaps then it is inevitable that Christians, including theologians, will speak in "various kinds of tongues"— which is not harmful, as Paul observed, so long as there are those standing by who can interpret the tongues, and so long as we realize that "all these are inspired by one and the same Spirit, who apportions to each one individually as he wills."

Notes for Essay 4

1 *Akt und Sein: Transzendentalphilosophie und Ontologie in der systematischen Theologie.* "Beiträge zur Förderung christlicher Theologie," Band 2, Heft 2 (Gütersloh, 1931). Reprinted as Band V of the series "Theologische Bücherei" (Munich: Chr. Kaiser Verlag, 1956). The subtitle was omitted in the English translation by Bernard Noble, *Act and Being* (London: William Collins' Sons and New York: Harper & Brothers, 1962).

2 Quoted from the interchange between Tillich and Niebuhr in the volume *The Theology of Paul Tillich,* edited by Charles W. Kegley and Robert W. Bretall (New York: The Macmillan Company, 1952), pp. 226 and 339. See also the continuation of the interchange in the same editors' later volume *Reinhold Niebuhr: His Religious, Social, and Political Thought* (New York: The Macmillan Company, 1956).

3 See, for example, the Anglo-Catholic E. L. Mascall's volume *The Recovery of Unity: A Theological Approach* (London: Longmans, Green, 1958), which in turn refers to other relevant literature. On Christology, see Joseph Sittler, "A Christology of Function," *Lutheran Quarterly,* VI (1954), 122-131; and on the doctrine of the church, Jean-Louis Leuba, *Institution und Ereignis* (Göttingen: Vandenhoeck & Ruprecht, 1957).

4 See "The Theology of Crisis and Its Attitude Toward Philosophy and Science," printed in English in Volume III of Bonhoeffer's *Gesammelte Schriften* (collected writings), Eberhard Bethge, ed. (Munich: Chr. Kaiser Verlag, 1960), pp. 110-126.

5 Luther's lectures on Romans were published only in 1908 after having been lost for almost four hundred years. See Wilhelm Pauck's introduction to his English translation of the lectures (Philadelphia: The Westminster Press, 1961), Library of Christian Classics, Vol. XV. Bonhoeffer quotes from this work at a half-dozen crucial points in his argument.

6 See, for example, Barth's chapter on Kant in his *Protestant Thought: From Rousseau to Ritschl,* Brian Cozens, tr. (New York: Harper & Brothers, 1959), which though first published in 1946 derives from his lectures of an earlier period.

7 Quoted from the article "Act Psychology" in Dagobert D. Runes, ed., *The Dictionary of Philosophy* (New York: Philosophical Library, n.d.).

8 *Act and Being,* p. 39.

9 *Act and Being*, Bernard Noble, tr. (New York: Harper & Brothers, 1962), p. 81. By permission.

10 Dietrich Bonhoeffer, *Act and Being*, Bernard Noble, tr. (New York, Harper & Brothers, 1962), pp. 90f. Italics of key sentence our own. All excerpts from *Act and Being* used in this essay are by permission of the publisher.

11 *Ibid.*, p. 31.

12 *Ibid.*, p. 32.

13 *Ibid.*, pp. 100, 104.

14 *Ibid.*, p. 5.

15 *Ibid.*, p. 109.

16 See excerpt in text to which Note 10 in this essay refers.

17 *Act and Being* (op. cit.), p. 111.

18 *Ibid.*, p. 121.

19 *Ibid.*, p. 128.

20 *Ibid.*, p. 133.

21 A. L. Reys, "The One God," in George D. Smith, ed., *The Teaching of the Catholic Church* (London: Burns & Oates, 2nd ed., 1952), pp. 81f. Bonhoeffer himself refers primarily to the work of the neo-Thomist theologian Erich Przywara, S.J., who, as he says, has restored the principle of analogy of being (*analogia entis*) "with methodological brilliance to the center of Catholic philosophy and dogmatics." Przywara had published major works in German during the 1920's and in 1927-1929 had been engaged in a dialogue with Karl Barth on the nature of the church. It is tempting to speculate that the immediate impetus for Bonhoeffer's formulation of the act-being problem may have come from this dialogue. The documents were published at the time in the periodical *Zwischen den Zeiten*; Karl Gerhard Steck has provided a summary and interpretation of the debate in his contribution to the volume *Antwort: Karl Barth zum siebzigsten Geburtstag* (Zurich: Evangelischer Verlag, 1956).

22 *Act and Being* (op. cit.), p. 68.

23 *Ibid.*

24 *Ibid.*, p. 163.

25 *Ibid.*, p. 164.

26 *Ibid.*, p. 131.

27 *Ibid.*, p. 72.

28 Cf. Bonhoeffer's comment in the section marking the transition from his analysis of philosophical treatments of his basic problem to his direct discussion of theology: "Nevertheless it may be that in the following pages we shall find in genuine transcendentalism and idealism . . . certain contributions to the solution of the act-being problem *within* revelation, if only because they have exhaustively fathomed and argued the philosophical dilemma of act and being" (*Act and Being* [op. cit.], p. 70).

Bonhoeffer's whole approach in *Act and Being* might also be taken to imply some such argument as the following: There are only a limited number of possible modes of thought (for example, thinking primarily in terms of continuity or primarily in terms of discontinuity). Theologies, too, fall into such modes; each theology is therefore correlatable with a philosophy of the same mode, and will benefit by an explicit dialogue with the same.

29 Cf. above, in the second paragraph preceding this one of the text.

Bonhoeffer also reflects Heidegger's stress on temporality when in the concluding sections of the book he interprets man's being in Adam and being in

Christ as his being "determined by the past" and "determined by the future," respectively. See *Act and Being (op. cit.)*, pp. 177-184.

31 *Act and Being (op. cit.)*, p. 64.

32 *Ibid.*, p. 65.

33 *Ibid.*, p. 37.

34 *Ibid.*, p. 142.

35 *Ibid.*, p. 150.

36 *Ibid.*, p. 143.

37 *Ibid.*, p. 150.

38 *Ibid.*, p. 151.

39 *Cf.* pp. 44-48, 105-107. Seeberg as professor of systematic theology at Berlin, had been the adviser for Bonhoeffer's doctoral thesis and sponsored his appointment as a lecturer.

40 *Act and Being (op. cit.)*, p. 16.

41 *Cf.* ftn. 2, p. 121, *Act and Being*.

42 *Act and Being (op. cit.)*, p. 27.

43 *Cf. Church Dogmatics*, Vol. III, Part 4 (Edinburgh: T. & T. Clark, 1961), pp. 16ff.

44 Karl Barth, *The Humanity of God*, John Newton Thomas and Thomas Wieser, trs. (Richmond, Va.: John Knox Press, 1960), p. 42. Used by permission.

45 Barth, "The Living Congregation of the Living Lord Jesus Christ," in *Man's Disorder and God's Design* (New York: Harper & Brothers, n.d.).

46 *Cf.* Hans Urs von Balthasar, *Karl Barth: Darstellung und Deutung seiner Theologie* (Cologne, 1951).

47 *Church Dogmatics*, Vol. I, Part I (Edinburgh: T. & T. Clark, 1936), p. ix.

48 From the essay "The Gift of Freedom" in *The Humanity of God (op. cit.)*, p. 92.

49 *Cf.* Paul Tillich, *Systematic Theology*, Vol. I (Chicago: University of Chicago Press, 1951), ftn. 13, pp. 50f.

5

The Source of Answers to the Question Concerning Jesus Christ

Most of the authors in this volume combine admiration for the achievement of Bonhoeffer with critical reservations and cautionary remarks concerning much of his methodology. In no chapter does this become more clear than in Professor Harrelson's dissection of Bonhoeffer's scriptural exegesis. As the young German theologian pursued the concreteness of revelation in Jesus Christ he found himself moving out of academy and into the world (of travel), the Church (of the expanding ecumenical movement) and the day-to-day parochial activities of his nation (with the secret seminaries). Most of all, the rise of the Nazi opposition to the Church forced on him the most primitive questions, necessitating the most direct and clear assertions. This situation led him—as it led other reformers before him—to expounding the Sacred Scriptures.

This he did with memorability (who can forget The Cost of Discipleship?), finesse, and most of all intensity. But if Peter Berger could suggest that Bonhoeffer's sociological endeavor would have been more successful had he chosen sociological tools more consistent with his goals, so, too, can Walter Harrelson point to some serious exegetical deficiencies. Bonhoeffer, who so strenuously urged that we must first listen to the page of Scripture did not, we find, rigorously discipline himself to do that. He brought more preconceptions than usual or necessary, and verged on allegorization of the Old Testament. The champion of the matter-of-fact worldliness of the Old Testament in his last letters tended to misinterpret it in his earlier exegetical work. Perhaps, suggests Harrelson, Bonhoeffer should be thought of as a homily maker and not an exegete at all. If his students can remember the same, not confusing the tools of the two crafts, they can profit immeasurably from Bonhoeffer's "divining" (to imply Dilthey's understanding) of Scripture.

Harrelson, who lauds the quest for concreteness in scriptural study is, by the way, uneasy with what he sees to be a dualism in Bonhoeffer's later approach to "nonreligious interpretation of Scripture." In the light of the general enthusiasm for the "nonreligious" project, Harrelson's strictures should be taken seriously.

The author of this essay teaches Old Testament at Vanderbilt Divinity School in Nashville, Tennessee; formerly he was Dean of the Divinity School at the University of Chicago. Educated in Europe and America, he is a member of a number of ecumenical biblical study commissions. The author of numerous technical articles in the field of Old Testament can be approached by readers of this book in his own simple and brief commentary on Jeremiah, a paperback from Judson Press. In his preface to that work for laymen, our author reveals his own intentions to be not far from Bonhoeffer's: "Biblical study should have one primary aim in view: confrontation of all of us by the living God. . . . With fear and trembling, we can dare to hope that God will address us through the biblical words. . . . No serious question is out of place. No pious phrases will take the place of honest and determined examination of the Bible."

Bonhoeffer and the Bible[1]

By Walter Harrelson

ALTHOUGH Bonhoeffer was primarily a theologian and a church-man rather than a specialist in biblical studies he devoted a sizable portion of his time and energy to the exposition of biblical themes and texts. His writings on the Bible may be classified roughly into three groups: (1) exegetical studies; (2) sermons; and (3) essays, letters, and papers dealing with biblical themes or texts. In this essay we shall first deal with the problem of Bonhoeffer's method of biblical interpretation and then examine briefly each of the three types of writing on the Bible.

Method

Bonhoeffer's lecture entitled "Vergegenwärtigung neutestamentlicher Texte," delivered on August 23, 1935, contains a good introduction to his method of biblical interpretation.[2] The term "Vergegenwärtigung" ("re-presentation") is used to designate the whole process by which the biblical message is presented to Church and world in a vital and meaningful way. It describes what we mean by the task and process of making the biblical Word relevant to contemporary man. Bonhoeffer distinguishes between a false and a correct meaning of the term. It is false, he says, to require the Bible to speak to our own ideas about God, man, and the world; to make our own ideas, desires, myths, world-views the norm of what is valuable and what is without value in the biblical record. Man must not set the questions for the Bible out of his own reason, experiences, desires, and hopes. He must not seek to justify the biblical message before a world which finds that message strange; to do so is to assume that the message is already the possession of the justifier. It is to make man the measure of the Gospel rather than to learn from the Gospel the true norm for human existence.

This false understanding of re-presentation is too much concerned with method and too little concerned with the biblical Word itself, says Bonhoeffer. The thirsty man will drink water from any sort of container; the contents is much more important to him than is the vessel, the container. True re-presentation involves not the justification of Christianity before the present generation (which Bonhoeffer accuses the German Christians, those who collaborated with Nazism, of doing) but the justification of the present world before the Christian message. The norm and standard of all re-presentation of the Gospel is Jesus Christ, witnessed to in the New Testament. All too often, says Bonhoeffer, we assume that the right movement is from the Bible to the contemporary world. But the true movement is from the present day to the Bible. We go to the Bible to discover what is meaningful for man, what man's problems are, what man's situation is in the world. We go to the Bible and there we remain. Exegesis is the fundamental way to make the biblical message real and helpful in any age.

Exegesis is not designed to enable us to extract from the Bible certain eternal truths. Bonhoeffer says that we can not distinguish the eternal from the temporal, we can not isolate essential biblical teachings, we can not separate the Word of God from the words of men. The whole Bible, in the fullness of its witness to God's Word, must be heard and heard out; and in these words—temporal, contingent, human words— God's Word Jesus Christ comes to us. The Holy Spirit makes the words of the Bible present to and for us—nothing and no one else. It is remarkable, says Bonhoeffer, that we always want to add something to the interpretation of the text, making it more concrete, more contemporary than it otherwise would be. But what can be more concrete, more contemporary than the biblical words themselves as they bear witness to Jesus Christ? Nothing needs to be added: no polemic against heretics, no specific application to specific situations. The right method for making the biblical message relevant to contemporary man is simply—exegesis!

In Bonhoeffer's other writings it is made clear that the *entire* Bible is to be interpreted in relation to Jesus Christ. The Old Testament is no less the Bible of the Church than is the New Testament. Traditional ways of relating Old and New Testaments are not satisfactory to Bonhoeffer (Law and Gospel, Promise and Fulfillment, Old Testament Messianic references, and the like). He insists that Christ is found in the Old as well as in the New Testament, and not alone in those passages which herald the coming of the Messiah.

Bonhoeffer's christological interpretation of the Old Testament appears in his earliest exegetical work, *Creation and Fall* (1933). There he says, for example, that God's creation of the world out of nothing (Genesis 1:1) is already the Gospel, Christ, the Resurrected One. "From the very beginning the world stands under the sign of the resurrection of Christ from the dead." [3] The christological references are even more explicit in Bonhoeffer's Bible study entitled "König David." [4] He interprets the entire career of David as lying under the shadow of Christ. Christ is in David, is present with him, the anointed king of Israel. David consorts with sinners and outcasts, he refuses to take action to wrest the royal power from Saul, he waits obediently and patiently for God's own action to prepare the way for his assumption of the throne. During the revolt of Absalom, David goes out of Jerusalem across the Kidron valley in humiliation and disgrace, just as the new

David, Jesus Christ, is later to go out to pray and to be betrayed. Bonhoeffer here interprets the Old Testament much in the manner of Wilhelm Vischer.[5]

Bonhoeffer's short study of the Psalms is also a christological interpretation.[6] Christ's presence in the Psalms is said to ratify these words of men as the Word of God. They are transformed into God's Word for man in that Christ prayed these prayers, making of man's words to God the Word of God for man. In the Psalter, David is said to be the author of many Psalms. But David the anointed king of Israel is the forerunner of Jesus Christ, Israel's true King. Christ himself prays in the prayers of David, and we who pray these prayers do so in the name of Christ.

The christological interpretation of the Old Testament appears in Bonhoeffer's sermons as well, as will be pointed out below. In the lecture on re-presentation he goes farther and offers a defense of the allegorical interpretation of Scripture, under certain limitations.[7] Explicit logical and grammatical meanings of a word or verse may not exhaust its meaning. The word may contain other perspectives of meaning also. When symbolic or allegorical meanings are found, however, they must point to Christ alone, and they must hold fast to the text itself. Symbolic or allegorical meanings must not be used to establish the unity of Scripture; the unity of Scripture is presupposed in Jesus Christ and neither requires nor allows of proof. Nor must allegorical interpretation take precedence over literal interpretation. But within such limits, symbolic or allegorical exposition can provide a fine example of the Church's freedom of biblical interpretation.

To sum up: Bonhoeffer interprets the entire Bible christologically. The Christian can not read the Old Testament as though Christ had not come. The Bible is the book of the Church; it can not adequately be understood without reference to the Lord of the Church. The interpreter uses various means to comprehend its meaning: such as philological, literary, historical. But the fundamental meaning of the Bible is Jesus Christ—and Christ reveals himself in the whole Bible to those who in faith turn to it. The reader comes to the Bible with no interpretive keys, no set of ideas of what the modern world must hear from the Bible, no theories of how or why its message is relevant for contemporary man. He turns to the Bible because Jesus Christ addresses him in the Bible's words. He expects to find Christ there, and in faith he does so. The one unifying reality which holds together the entire Bible is Jesus Christ the Word made flesh.

Our critical appraisal of Bonhoeffer's method will be given in more detail below, as we analyze his several types of writing on the Bible. Here we need only say that Bonhoeffer's christological interpretation of the Old Testament seems to us to be unnecessary. Would it not have been more consistent for Bonhoeffer to have argued that the Bible may or may not bear witness to Christ? Why should he not have summoned us to do our exegesis with no key at all, not even the christological key to the Bible's meaning? Is Bonhoeffer not violating his own warning that we bring nothing to the Bible save our own readiness to hear God address us? Is he not insisting upon a dogmatic presupposition that only in Jesus Christ may man know God? Is such a presupposition defensible?

Exegetical Works

Bonhoeffer's two chief exegetical works—neither of them exegetical in the ordinary meaning of the term—are Creation and Fall (1933), published in English translation in 1959, and The Cost of Discipleship (1937), which appeared in English in 1948. Other exegetical studies include the following: "König David," published in 1936; "Der Wiederaufbau Jerusalems nach Esra und Nehemia," [8] which appeared in the same year; and Das Gebetbuch der Bibel (1940). Two shorter works should also be mentioned: Temptation, a series of Bible studies delivered in 1937 which were edited by Eberhard Bethge and first published in 1953, the English translation appearing in 1955; and "*Dein Reich komme*," first published in 1933 and reprinted in 1957 together with another study, "*Die erste Tafel, eine Auslegung der ersten drei Gebote*," written in 1944.[9] Several other Bible studies have also appeared in the edition of Bonhoeffer's collected works.[10]

Creation and Fall was Bonhoeffer's major exegetical effort. In it he makes a clear break with his colleagues at Berlin, where the lectures were given in 1932-1933. His existentialist theology, dependent upon Karl Barth to a considerable extent, is clearly in evidence in this book. He speaks, for example, of man's living in relation to the center of existence, symbolized by the tree of life in the Garden of Eden. Man lives in freedom, which means that he lives in the garden guiltless, obedient without knowing that he is obedient. He is free *for* God and neighbor, free *from* bondage to any other creature inasmuch as he is appointed to rule over all other creatures. Man's knowledge of good and evil which comes after he has eaten from the fruit forbidden him is knowledge of death; it is in fact his death. To be dead means no longer to live before God and yet to be required to live before God; it means to have life no longer as a gift but as a commandment. To be dead means to be required to live.

These traces of the author's existentialist thought are pointed out only to indicate that Bonhoeffer—departing from his own method—*has* brought something to the text other than Jesus Christ. This existentialist philosophical theology, which Bonhoeffer later abandoned, is a powerful exegetical instrument in his hands. What he has to say about Genesis 1-3 is highly illuminating and often quite original. It is a good thing for his exegesis, in fact, that he comes to the text with this particular interpretive key. And quite apart from this existentialism he has cast light upon the familiar text at many points.

Bonhoeffer maintains that the text speaks of creation out of nothing. His discussion of nothingness in connection with Genesis 1:1-2 (also a mark of his existentialist thinking) is keen and helpful, but it is not exegesis. Genesis 1 speaks of God's sovereign freedom in the act of creation, but it does not speak of creation out of nothing. Bonhoeffer's treatment of sexuality seems to me to be dead wrong, entirely untrue to the meaning of sexuality in these chapters (chapters 2-3) and in the Old Testament in general. Sexuality does not mean annihilation through creativity, not even in a fallen world. As one element of man's existence in sin, it too is marked by sin. But Bonhoeffer goes much farther than this and leaves the Scripture behind him as he does so.

Bonhoeffer's references to Christ in this study seem to me to be gratuitous. If the biblical passage is simply a point of departure for a theological exposition of the meaning of creation and fall in Christian thinking, then the christological references are appropriate. But Bonhoeffer is intent upon exegesis, quite clearly, and there is no warrant for the references to Christ in an exegetical study of a passage in which Christ simply is not the subject of concern. Exegesis deals with what a text says, with its contents as these contents took shape in the period which produced the text. If we insist upon an approach to Scripture which requires the text to speak to us, to our problems and our understandings, are we not doing precisely what Bonhoeffer warns us not to do? If we are to go beyond the meaning of the text for Israel, should we not distinguish this Christian import of the text from its meaning for the community in which the text first took shape? [11]

We turn now to Bonhoeffer's other major exegetical study. *The Cost of Discipleship* is an examination of discipleship, divided into four parts. The first deals with Jesus' call to his disciples and what it means to obey that call. The second part is an exposition of portions of the Sermon on the Mount. In the third part Bonhoeffer examines themes taken from Jesus' sending of his disciples on the mission to Israel (Matthew

9:35-10:42). The fourth part is on the Church and discipleship, in relation to some passages and themes from Paul's letters. This outline of the work indicates that Bonhoeffer is not
here engaged in exegesis in the ordinary sense of the term, just
as he was not in his work on creation and fall. This is Bible
study, presented in the form of a series of *homilies* on the
texts. In one of his lectures to the Finkenwalde seminar for
preachers he spoke with high praise of the homily as a form
of biblical exposition: "The homily is the most exacting and
at the same time the most appropriate form of interpretation
of the text." [12] These homilies are masterful examples of Bible
study which aims to bring the reader and the hearer directly
into the circle of Jesus' hearers and disciples. Bonhoeffer moves
unselfconsciously from the first to the twentieth century and
back again. The brilliance and the seriousness of Bonhoeffer's
exposition of these familiar New Testament passages are un-
mistakable and beyond praise.

Here again, however, we must ask whether Bonhoeffer is
faithful to his methodological guides. *The Cost of Discipleship*
is dominated throughout by Bonhoeffer's own program for the
Confessing Church of his day. He has brought with him, that
is to say, a particular understanding of the Church, of the relation between Church and State, of the necessity for the reform
of Church and society in his own time. What he has to say
about the necessity for the Church to live in the world for the
sake of Christ, rather than for the sake of the world, reflects
one strand—but only one strand—of the New Testament message on this point. This is not intended as a criticism of the
book; on the contrary, the book is all the better for Bonhoeffer's not having come to the text free of these presuppositions.
The point is only that this New Testament study is done by
one who knows at the start what he is looking for; he comes to
the text with more than "Jesus Christ alone"—as everyone
does.

The entire work is a call to discipleship, to obedience. Without obedience, faith is empty. Christ must be followed, without qualification, without excuses, at the cost of one's life. "When Christ calls a man, he bids him come and die." [13] This is the theme of Bonhoeffer's remarkable study. The author's own heroic obedience to death makes it difficult for one to criticize this work. But Bonhoeffer would be the first to insist that his work be evaluated critically.

Bonhoeffer only occasionally makes explicit use of the findings of critical scholars. He goes his own way in the interpretation of the Gospels. Only rarely does he indicate that we may not have Jesus' own words in the Gospel records. Seldom does he distinguish between the Synoptic and Johannine Gospels; both are used as equally reliable records of Jesus' words and deeds. A church theologian is here writing for the Church. Much knowledge of critical issues is presupposed on the part of his readers, much goes unsaid, in the interest of calling the Church of Jesus Christ to concrete acts of obedience to its Lord.

Here are some of the points Bonhoeffer makes in this set of homilies: The Church must learn again that it lives by unswerving allegiance to its Lord and by no other way. The path of suffering and rejection is its only proper path. The Church can not expect to be understood by the world, nor can it expect to be tolerated for long by the world if it is really the Church. A select few of its members may be called to the highest path of obedience—martyrdom. The Church, Bonhoeffer says, must not cast its pearls before swine. It must keep its treasures safe from defilement. Its members must live a life of rigorous discipline, recognizing that their works of righteousness contribute nothing to their justification by God, but demonstrating in and before the world that they live through the power of the crucified and risen Lord of world and Church. The Sermon on the Mount, for example, is represented to be the literal word of Jesus which the disciples are summoned to fulfill in their own lives. To be sure, only Jesus Christ himself fulfills this commandment of the Kingdom, but he calls all who follow him to recognize that *this* is his word to them, his call to obedience in discipleship.

This discipleship is precisely the work of the Church which holds the world together. This is the light of the world, the salt of the earth. The Church is all this because the Church is one with Christ and he one with it. "Through his Spirit, the crucified and risen Lord exists as the Church, as the new man," [14] although Christ is at the same time the Lord, the Head of the Church. The Church is not to be surprised or overwhelmed by suffering or rejection by the world, for "the messengers of Jesus will be hated to the end of time." [15] It is to persevere in its witness, holding fast to Jesus Christ and his Word, living in the fellowship of his Body until his return in glory.

Bonhoeffer's call to the Church to be itself and to live only from the strength provided by its crucified and risen Lord is not merely a tract for the times of persecution, a message the validity of which applied only during the days of the struggle of the Confessing Church with Nazism and with the German Christians. This is a study of enduring value. Nor should readers be put off by the apparently naïve biblicism found here. Bonhoeffer knew very well what he was doing, what he was leaving unsaid. Yet the fact remains that this study can not be called adequate exegesis of the texts treated. It is a dangerous piece of writing on the New Testament because the author's intention and method can so easily be misunderstood.

For one thing, *The Cost of Discipleship* can be read as a sectarian tract, as a call for the Church to "get back to the Bible" and follow its injunctions just as they stand, without regard to changing circumstances or fresh calls to obedience. How easy it would be, for example, to defend quietism, passivity before evil, from the following words: "The only way to overcome evil is to let it run itself to a standstill because it does not find the resistance it is looking for." [16] But it would be possible to make this word into a purely spiritual counsel should we accept the quotation found a few lines later: "To make non-resistance a principle for secular life is to deny God, by undermining his gracious ordinance for the preservation of the world." [17] A very subtle theological thinker is at work in this apparently simple marshaling of the New Testament evidence on discipleship.

More serious is Bonhoeffer's bypassing of literary and historical study of the New Testament. Why did he not make it clearer to readers that enormously complex problems face us as we seek to know what Jesus' call to discipleship actually is? Is it responsible New Testament exegesis to imply that Jesus knew from the start of his ministry that he was destined to die on the cross? Is the story of the sending of the disciples (Matthew 10) historical? Do we have, or can we recover by any means whatever, the original words of Jesus? Bonhoeffer had the courage to ignore all these questions, to write a book which he knew would be attacked as unscientific. It was for him an example of scientific theological exegesis,[18] and this judgment can of course be defended; but it is still perilous to suggest even by implication that the Church has such direct access to Jesus' words and deeds as Bonhoeffer appears to suggest.

Despite these criticisms, it must be said that perhaps no one else in all Christendom could have written this marvelous call to Christian discipleship. The truth, the power, the magnificent insights of *The Cost of Discipleship* make it worth reading and rereading. Like the Bible itself, it is a book with which one must wrestle, to which one frequently takes exception, but which always casts illumination upon the Bible, the Church today, the world in which we live, and upon one's own discipleship.

Bonhoeffer's other biblical studies, illuminating though they are, also raise many problems. His study of David [19] seems to be the worst of the lot. The biblical record of David's life and work is marked by a subtle ambiguity: was David an extremely shrewd politician who knew how to turn every situation to his own advantage, or was he the faithful and obedient servant of God portrayed by Bonhoeffer? Bonhoeffer never once suggests that the former interpretation has any warrant from the text itself, and yet it seems entirely clear that the author of the tradition of the succession to David's throne (II Samuel 9-20; I Kings 1-2) has presented David in such a way as to allow for either interpretation. The fact may be that David was *both* a clever schemer *and* a pious worshiper of Yahweh. Bonhoeffer's treatment of David is not only questionable from the point of view of his christological interpretation; it is also inadequate as an account of how the Bible itself presents David to its readers.

The study of Ezra and Nehemiah [20] is clearly an effort to make the Bible speak to the situation of the Church struggle in Germany. No literary or historical problems are discussed, although the books of Ezra and Nehemiah bristle with literary and historical difficulties. Bonhoeffer points out that the enemies of the Church in the days of Ezra and Nehemiah have two alternative ways by which to destroy the Church. First they seek the way of collaboration: "Let us build with you!" (Ezra 4:2). When they are refused a place in the building operation, their hostility quickly becomes manifest. Now they attack the Church outright and seek to destroy it. But their efforts fail. The Church is re-established by God, and it is cleansed by the exercise of church discipline—an absolutely necessary action, hard though it be upon those who must carry it through.

This brief study given in 1936 to the seminar for preachers in Finkenwalde is of course not presented as a full-scale exegetical study of Ezra and Nehemiah. Bonhoeffer presupposes a knowledge of the literary and historical problems on the part of his university-trained hearers. He is seeking to enable them to enter more fully into the meaning of the Church's Scripture, interpreted christologically, to show them that the Bible speaks directly to problems faced by the Church in any time or situation. Here again we have a homily on the text, not an exegetical study. Its meaning for the Confessing Church in Bonhoeffer's day is obvious. It should also be clear, however, that Bonhoeffer has dealt with only a few issues raised by the books of Ezra and Nehemiah, and that it would be a tragic misunderstanding of Bonhoeffer's intention should his method be viewed as the only correct way to study these biblical books. Bonhoeffer's method is a far cry from the method of the Scofield Bible!

The remainder of Bonhoeffer's exegetical works must be left aside, although his treatment of the Psalms will be referred to briefly in the section immediately following. Our further criticism of his christological approach also appears in this next section.

Sermons

Bonhoeffer's sermons may well contain his best exegetical work. He followed quite faithfully the advice he gave to preachers in his lectures on homiletics delivered at Finkenwalde during the years 1935-1939.[21] He chose texts rich in content, full of exegetical difficulties, often incapable of adequate treatment in a single sermon. He began immediately with the text, avoiding long introductions, coming quickly to the heart of the text. He moved through the entire text, letting his exposition of the text bear the weight of relevancy, not seeking for a point of contact with contemporary life in church or society.

From the collection of sermons which have been published [22] we select two for a brief examination of his exegetical method. The first is an exposition of Matthew 18:21-35, preached on November 7, 1935.[23] Bonhoeffer begins by asking the congregation whether its members can think of anyone whom they have not forgiven. Should they be tempted to say right away that they know of no one, he reminds them how strange it would be if they were really able to say this, and what a surprise might await all of us should those arise whom we have not forgiven and bear witness against us: those whom we had not taken seriously as persons but simply ignored, those whose lives we had not borne up, whom we had not stood by in their times of need.

Peter's question to Jesus, Bonhoeffer says, is a serious one. Are there not after all limits to forgiveness? Must we keep on forgiving, as much as seven times? Really to forgive seven times is no simple matter. But Jesus' response is that we are not permitted to count, to keep score, in our acts of forgiveness. We are to forgive without end. "Free yourself from counting, Peter; forgiving and pardoning know no number or end; you need not trouble yourself over your own right in the matter, since that is covered by God; you may forgive without end. Forgiveness is without beginning and end, it takes place daily and unceasingly, for it comes from God." [24]

Yet we can hardly keep from raising objections, Bonhoeffer grants. Surely the time comes when we must insist upon our own rights and hold the one who has wronged us accountable for his wrong. In response to this human reaction Jesus tells the parable of the unforgiving servant (Matthew 18:23-35). How forgetful we are! We forget the mercy of God who in Jesus Christ has forgiven us all, has not held us accountable for our sin and rebellion but has laid all our sin upon Jesus— yet we heartlessly hold out for our right against one who has done some little injustice to us. The text calls us "to participate in bearing the distress of the brother, to serve, to help, to forgive—without measure, without qualification, without end." [25]

No word of criticism or commendation is in order here. Bonhoeffer has opened the text to hearers and readers and has let it speak its own inescapable word. The same is not the case, in my judgment, with our second example. This sermon is an exposition of Psalm 58.[26] The bitter cry for vengeance contained in the psalm has caused trouble to Christians and Jews throughout the centuries. Is the spirit of vengefulness here expressed not unworthy to have a place in the Bible? Can a Christian pray such a prayer?

Bonhoeffer grants that a Christian can not pray this prayer. He is stopped from praying it not because he is too good to express such sentiments but because he is too sinful to do so. Only the sinless one, only the perfectly righteous one may pray this prayer: David—or rather, Christ in David. David was not without sin, but he was chosen to bear witness to the new David, Jesus Christ. Christ prays this prayer. His innocence goes out in the world and charges those who do evil, who deal out violence on earth, whose venom is like that of the serpent.

Christ prays for the destruction of evil, for the rooting out of all opposition to God's will and purpose. Christ himself also destroys evil in his own death and resurrection. Those made righteous in Christ rejoice in the blood of Christ shed for the sins of the world. They bathe their feet in this blood shed by the one who was made sin, made wickedness for them, that they might share in the reward of the righteous.

There is no denying that Bonhoeffer's sermon goes to the center of the Christian affirmation, that the Gospel is here proclaimed with power and vitality. But what are we to make of this understanding of the psalm, of this use of it in Christian proclamation? Must we not grant that there was once an Israelite who prayed this prayer for vengeance against his adversaries? And that other Israelites with him—not sinless men —poured out this understandable prayer to God that God vindicate his righteousness publicly? If the Christian wishes to say that Christ only can pray this prayer, must he not also admit that others have prayed it—and that Christians have prayed such prayers through the ages?

This is not, however, the most serious point, in my judgment. More important is the fact that here, as often in his exegesis, Bonhoeffer simply removes the Bible of the Jews from their hands. If the Old Testament has no meaning for faith apart from its meaning in Jesus Christ, then those who—in faith—do not declare Jesus to be the Messiah are simply left without their Scripture, are they not? I know of no writing of Bonhoeffer which seeks to lay out the relation between Judaism and Christianity.[27] His entire life is ample testimony to his readiness to fight for the rights of the Jews as citizens, on theological grounds, and against the monstrous measures taken by the Nazi regime against them. But what of his rigorous christological interpretation of the Old Testament? Is it defensible to say without qualification that the prayer book of the Bible—the Psalms—is prayed by Jesus and thus made into the Word of God? [28] Christ is in David, we hear in Bonhoeffer's study of the Psalms, but clearly he is not the one who the author of Psalm 58 believed was praying this prayer for vengeance. Was the prayer then without meaning until Christ came? Is it without meaning for the Jew who does not today name Jesus Christ as Lord? Does the Jew know nothing of the meaning of creation and fall because he does not declare that this meaning is given from the End, from Jesus Christ? Is King David without significance for the Jewish community because it does not see in him the shadow and prefiguration of Christ?

It is impossible to believe that Bonhoeffer intended this conclusion to be drawn. Apparently he would have distinguished the Israelite *understanding* of the Old Testament from the *truth* of the Old Testament witness to Jesus Christ. The one God appeared in the person of Jesus of Nazareth the Christ. The Christian must simply speak the truth: that God bore witness to himself in Israel; that in Jesus Christ the same God appears among men; that therefore the triune God of Christian faith who is known fully in Jesus Christ is also witnessed to in Israel, in the Old Testament. The early Christians saw in their Scripture (the Old Testament) a witness to Christ; can later Christians deny this testimony of the early Church?

This rejoinder would answer only a part of the problem. The fact still remains that Bonhoeffer, if we take his words at face value, does not assign much meaning to the faith and hope of Israel for Israel, or for the Jewish people today. The unity of the Bible is given only in Jesus Christ; only in Christ is David understood; only in Christ is creation understood; only in Christ are the prayers of men in the Psalter also the Word of God to man. This seems to me to be entirely unjustified, exegetically and theologically. Given this understanding of the meaning of the life and faith of Israel, Bonhoeffer can persist in portraying Judaism in New Testament times in a way which is patently erroneous. In *The Cost of Discipleship* he says, among other things, that in Jesus' day "there were no longer any shepherds in Israel. No one led the flock to fresh waters to quench their thirst, no one protected them from the wolf. They were harassed, wounded, and distraught under the dire rod of their shepherds, and lay prostrate upon the ground. Such was the condition of the people when Jesus came." [29] This judgment is presented as though it were historical fact, as though it properly described the situation within Judaism in Jesus' day. The one-sidedness of this judgment has long been recognized and acknowledged—although all too many interpreters of the New Testament still lapse back into this palpably erroneous picture as they write. In fact, it seems clear that Bonhoeffer sees in Judaism nothing more than a religion —the religion of the Elect People, to be sure. It is a religion of the Law; hence he can speak about the necessity for a mission to the Jews without qualification.[30] It was not necessary, however, for the Dead Sea Scrolls to be discovered in order for us to know better than this. German scholars had themselves done much of the work which placed Judaism in New Testament times in a much clearer light than that gained from the New Testament alone (Schürer, Billerbeck, and others).

It is the more surprising that Bonhoeffer fails to give the Old Testament its relative autonomy as a part of the Bible of the Church in the light of his undoubted love for Old Testament literature and his stress upon the concreteness of revelation there portrayed. Not even in his letters from prison does he alter his fundamental judgment concerning the Old Testament, although he has many affirmative things to say about it in the letters. Bonhoeffer's approach to the Old Testament did enable him to help to preserve the Old Testament as Christian Scripture, against those who would have eliminated it. But he rescued it for the Church by denying it to Israel. I find it intolerable to maintain that the Jews who went to their death in Buchenwald and Dachau were in any less favorable position to comprehend the meaning of God's redemptive love, witnessed to in their Scripture, than were Bonhoeffer and his fellow Christian martyrs. Bonhoeffer certainly would not maintain such a view. Yet it is possible to gain such an inference from the rigorous christological interpretation of the Old Testament which he displays in his exegetical work and in the sermon under discussion.[31]

Bonhoeffer's sermons are masterful examples of exegetical preaching, showing the concreteness of revelation in the biblical Word. They get directly to the center of Christian faith quickly and they carry the hearer into the text and through it to the end. His concern to speak directly and concretely to the Church from the Bible lies behind all that he did in biblical studies. With the possible exception of *Creation and Fall* all his biblical studies are in the tradition of the homily, are more sermons than exegetical studies. Specialists in biblical exegesis may shake their heads over Bonhoeffer's exegetical method, over the many problems passed by in silence, over what seems to be childish naïveté at many points. But they (the present writer included) might bear in mind that Bonhoeffer closes his book *Akt und Sein* with the reminder that the Christian is summoned to become a child.[32]

Letters and Papers

Here we shall deal only with the letters and papers from prison, since these are held to mark a great transition in Bonhoeffer's understanding both of the nature of the biblical message and of the way in which it is to be presented in a world come of age. We restrict our remarks to two problems: (1) Bonhoeffer's new (or apparently new) understanding of the significance of the Old Testament; and (2) the question whether Bonhoeffer's call for a secular interpretation of biblical terminology is itself defensible biblical interpretation.

On the first question, it is clear that Bonhoeffer's view of the meaning of Old Testament faith does undergo change. In my judgment, the change is not so great as some interpreters have supposed. He argues in a letter of June 27, 1944, that the New Testament is no more a religion of redemption from the world than is the Old. The Old Testament speaks of *historical* redemption, redemption on this side of death. The resurrection hope in the New Testament is not an other-worldly solution of the problems of this world; on the contrary, this hope "sends a man back to his life on earth in a wholly new way which is even more sharply defined than it is in the Old Testament." [33] Bonhoeffer's appreciation of the place of history in the Old Testament picture of revelation is here disclosed, but this had been stressed very clearly and strongly by Eichrodt, Koehler, and Barth prior to this time. But his comments about the New Testament meaning of resurrection are striking and represent a departure from his prior exegetical work.

Bonhoeffer's celebrated comment about the name of God in the Old Testament in relation to Jesus Christ is quite ambiguous:

It is only when one knows the ineffability of the Name of God that one can utter the name of Jesus Christ. It is only when one loves life and the world so much that without them everything would be gone, that one can believe in the resurrection and a new world. It is only when one submits to the law that one can speak of grace, and only when one sees the anger and wrath of God hanging like grim realities over the head of one's enemies that one can know something of what it means to love them and forgive them.[34]

Here Bonhoeffer sees Old Testament faith to represent the "next to last" thing and the New Testament to be the "last." The Old Testament view of the ineffability of God's name could be understood to reflect Israel's refusal to treat the holy God lightly, or it could represent Israel's dependence upon the Church for a name of God which it could make its own. I fear that here Bonhoeffer is saying that the Old Testament witnesses to man's need of redemption rather than to God the Redeemer. That is, the New Testament knows the name of the Redeemer; the Old Testament portrays man in his longing for redemption. The lies, cursings, blasphemies, adulteries, sins in the Old Testament, absent from the New Testament (!), to which Bonhoeffer refers in this letter, also suggest that God in the Old Testament is known only as the God of Law, of wrath, of promised grace.

The letter of April 30, 1944, also reflects Bonhoeffer's renewed appreciation of the concreteness of revelation in the Old Testament and in the New.[35] Here for the first time he speaks about the world which has "come of age," about the new secularity characteristic of Western European society. How does the Church live and bear its witness in such a world? It does so, first of all, by living fully and wholly in the world, asking no special consideration for itself, living as one secular institution among all the others, abdicating all official standing in the eyes of state and society. It also lives by means of its secret discipline, with its essential treasures guarded from the world, its prayers and acts of worship done quietly, unostentatiously, secretly. The Church moves out fully into the world living in obedience to Christ who suffers in and for the world. But it also lives by Word and Sacrament. The Old Testament provides ample warrant for the life of faith in the world, in the center of life—as does the New also. Bonhoeffer wants to see the Church stand "not where human powers give out, on the borders, but in the centre of the village. This is the way it is in the Old Testament, and in this sense we still read the New Testament far too little on the basis of the Old." [36] He says that he "should like to speak of God not on the borders of life but at its centre, not in weakness but in strength, not, therefore, in man's suffering and death but in his life and prosperity. On the borders it seems to me better to hold our peace and leave the problems unsolved."

This eloquent call for a robust and vital life in relationship to the world is clearly based upon Bonhoeffer's increasing love and appreciation for Old Testament faith. The Old Testament now seems to have a strong place in its own right in the Church, as a corrective to an inadequate or erroneous reading of the New Testament. Over and again in his letters Bonhoeffer refers to Jeremiah 45, to the word of Yahweh to Baruch: "Do you seek great things for yourself? Seek them not . . . nevertheless I am giving you your life as a prize of war in all places to which you go." The life of faith is life gained through living, through struggle, warfare. Christ is present in the warfare; one need not always speak of his presence or display faith in his presence through religious words or acts. God's promise to man is life and blessing and well-being in this world. God must not be relegated to a corner, nor must we seek desperately to make a place for him in a world which gets along quite nicely without reference to God. We must learn from the Bible, and especially from the Old Testament, that God lives and works at the center of man's existence, not on the periphery of existence.

On the second question—whether Bonhoeffer's call for a

secular interpretation of biblical terminology is itself faithful
to the biblical witness—the situation seems far from clear.
Bonhoeffer indicates his dissatisfaction with Bultmann's program of demythologization because it does not go far enough.
God and miracles can not be separated, but both must be
interpreted nonreligiously, Bonhoeffer maintains. Barth's
method does not work, he says, because he presents the whole
of biblical imagery to contemporary man and says, "Take it
or leave it." This is wrong on two counts, according to the
author. Man in a religionless world can not "take it." Moreover, it is wrong because the mysteries of Christian faith are
not thereby preserved from profanation in such a world.[37] I
find here a kind of dualism in Bonhoeffer's program. He wants
to find a way to present Christian faith by means of nonreligious equivalents of such terms as repentance, faith, justification, rebirth, sanctification. But he also wants the Church to
live a secret life in which the mystery of Word and Sacrament
is secured from profanation. The Church, on this view, lives
two lives—one public and the other private. This dualism is
far more dangerous, in my view, than the "positivism of revelation" of Barth (if that view of Barth be accepted) or the
"not far enough" of Bultmann.[38]

Bonhoeffer wants to "reclaim for Christ a world which has
come of age." [39] He will have nothing to do with the effort to
convince healthy men that they are really sick and in need of
the Gospel, nor with the practice of prying into the privacy
of men's lives to drag up their secret sins in order to show them
their need. God must not be relegated to some last, secret place
in men's hearts. Religious man, Christian man must recognize
that the world can and does get along without the hypothesis
that God exists. We must learn to live in the world as though
God did not in fact exist. Simple honesty requires that we do
so. "Before God and with him we live without God. God
allows himself to be edged out of the world and on to the
cross. God is weak and powerless in the world, and that is

exactly the way, the only way, in which he can be with us and help us." The Bible directs man to the "powerlessness and suffering of God; only a suffering God can help." This, says Bonhoeffer, "must be the starting point for our 'worldly' interpretation." [40]

How, then, does one live in a secular world?

> He must therefore plunge himself into the life of a god-less world, without attempting to gloss over its ungodliness with a veneer of religion or trying to transfigure it. He must live a "worldly" life and so participate in the suffering of God. He may live a worldly life as one emancipated from all false religions and obligations. To be a Christian means . . . to be a man. It is not some religious act which makes a Christian what he is, but participation in the suffering of God in the life of the world. . . . Jesus does not call men to a new religion, but to life. [41]

The Christian is to live this secular life while always trusting completely in God, participating in his sufferings, watching with Christ in Gethsemane. [42]

Bonhoeffer was not given the time to indicate the approach to be followed in his nonreligious interpretation of Christian faith. [43] He longed for public debate on the matter. "The Church must get out of her stagnation. We must move out again into the open air of intellectual discussion with the world, and risk shocking people if we are to cut any ice." [44] He sketched the outline of a book he wished to write on the subject, but on the matter of nonreligious language it is very sketchy indeed. [45] It is clear, however, that the dualism referred to above was still in his mind. The Church is not to cast its pearls before swine. Its inner life around Word and Sacrament would, it appears, provide its real sustenance in a religionless world, enabling the Christian to live his life of participation in the suffering of God in the world and enabling the Church to be ignored by society and claim no place of honor for itself. This seems to me to be the weakest point in Bonhoeffer's program.

The attack by Bonhoeffer, and by Barth before him, on religion has its clear warrant in the Bible. At the same time, it can not be denied that the Old and the New Testament display a faith which did and does find expression in what is called a religion. The important biblical point is that both Old and New Testament faith preserved room for the assault upon religion, upon the very religious forms in which this faith was expressed. This is the truth in the distinction drawn between biblical faith and religion. The ultimate reality for biblical man is the holy God himself, in his sovereign freedom, creating, preserving, redeeming, judging the world, including especially the *religious* world.

Must it not also be said that a nonreligious interpretation of biblical faith would soon become another religion, another form within which biblical faith was enshrined? This is for me the pathos in the call of Bonhoeffer for a secular reinterpretation of biblical terminology. Biblical faith would have undergone only one more effort of men to interpret its meaning in another set of terms. The nonreligious age which the Western world has entered does of course have its important differences from other ages, but it is not so different from other ages as to require, or to allow for, the break with religion which Bonhoeffer proposes. Should the program be realized, we should soon see another religion—a *nonreligious* religion—with its new terminology, its new cultic acts, its fresh set of ethical and cultural understandings and mandates. But the effort is still profoundly worthwhile. We may be sure that biblical faith as recast will provide the power and the incentive for the destruction of that new nonreligious religion should the time and need arise. The living God sees to his Word—as Bonhoeffer has enabled all of us the more firmly to believe.

This study has led to the conclusion that Bonhoeffer's greatest contributions to Christian theology do not lie in the area of biblical exegesis. The greatness of Bonhoeffer is to be found in his work on ethics, Christology, and the relation of Christian faith to contemporary society. It seems to be clear, nonetheless, that Bonhoeffer's profound wrestling with the Bible has been of central importance in the development of his thought in these areas. We may not have learned from him too much about the task and method of full-scale exegetical work on the Bible, but this is not what he was attempting to teach us in any case. We can learn from him that God still comes to us as He did in biblical times: concretely, in specific events, in the midst of our joys, sorrows, perplexities, faith, and doubt. Bonhoeffer could guide us through his homilies on biblical themes and texts to a day of renewed vitality in preaching and Bible study. In short, he could teach us to learn to live and to die with the biblical Word in our hands. Should we ask for more?

Notes for Essay 5

1 An illuminating essay on this subject appeared in *Die Mündige Welt*, I (1955), 62-76, written by Richard Grunow.

2 Dietrich Bonhoeffer, *Gesammelte Schriften* (Munich: Chr. Kaiser Verlag, 1958-1961), III (1960), 303-324.

3 Dietrich Bonhoeffer, *Creation and Fall*, John C. Fletcher, tr. (New York: The Macmillan Company, 1959), p. 16.

4 *Gesammelte Schriften* (*op. cit.*), IV (1961), 294-320.

5 See Vischer's *The Witness of the Old Testament to Christ* (London: Lutterworth Press, 1934, 1949).

6 *Das Gebetbuch der Bibel* (1940), also published in *Gesammelte Schriften*, IV, 544-569. See also his "Christus in den Psalmen," *Gesammelte Schriften*, III (1960), 294-302.

7 *Gesammelte Schriften* (*op. cit.*), IV, 319-320, and the editor's note to p. 320.

8 *Ibid.*, IV (1961), 321-335.

9 *Ibid.*, III (1960), 270-285; IV (1961), 597-612.

10 See especially *Gesammelte Schriften* (*op. cit.*), III, 325-381; IV, 183-236, 344-384, 466-543, 570-620.

11 Bonhoeffer grants that Adam can hardly be expected to know of the full meaning of what has happened to him, but no clear distinction is drawn between the meaning of the text in Israelite life and faith and its meaning for Christian faith. See p. 111 (3rd ed., 1955).

12 *Gesammelte Schriften* (*op. cit.*), IV, 269.

13 *The Cost of Discipleship*, Reginald Fuller, tr. (New York: The Macmillan Company, 1959), 2nd ed., p. 79.

14 *Ibid.*, p. 218. See *Sanctorum Communio* for the definition of the Church as "Christ existing as community."

15 *Ibid.*, p. 192.

16 *Ibid.*, p. 127.

17 *Ibid.*, p. 130.

18 See *Gesammelte Schriften* (*op. cit.*), II (1959), 369.

19 "König David," *Gesammelte Schriften* (*op. cit.*), IV (1961), 294-320.

20 *Ibid.*, IV (1961), 321-335.

21 *Ibid.*, IV (1961), 237-289.

22 *Gesammelte Schriften (op. cit.)*, IV (1961).

23 *Ibid.*, pp. 399-406.

24 *Ibid.*, p. 403.

25 *Ibid.*, p. 406.

26 *Ibid.*, pp. 413-422.

27 His lecture, *"Die Kirche vor der Judenfrage,"* delivered in April, 1933, is published in *Gesammelte Schriften*, II (1959), 44-53. Here he does make some observations about the continuing curse which lies upon the "elect people" for their crucifixion of the Redeemer of the world. The Church has never forgotten, he says, that Israel must bear the curse of its deed through a long history of suffering (although God alone exercises that curse; men are not to lay it upon Israel; see *Gesammelte Schriften*, II, 1959, p. 116). But the Jewish question must be understood religiously, not politically. The Jewish Christian is not a baptized convert to Christianity but one who holds to the Law rather than to Jesus Christ alone. Those who wish to expel Jewish converts from the Church are *themselves* the Jewish Christians.

This essay comes early in Bonhoeffer's theological life. His comments on the curse laid upon Israel (not without justification, to be sure, in the New Testament) should perhaps be mercifully forgotten.

28 See *Gesammelte Schriften (op. cit.)*, IV, 544-569; see especially 546-550.

29 Reprinted with the permission of the publisher from "The Harvest" in *The Cost of Discipleship*, p. 179, by Dietrich Bonhoeffer, tr. by Reginald Fuller. 2nd Rev. Ed. Copyright 1959 by The Macmillan Company.

30 See the references in Note 27 above.

31 The work of Wilhelm Vischer is much more responsible "christological" exegesis, for the most part, than is that of Bonhoeffer, in my judgment. See his *The Witness of the Old Testament to Christ* (1949). And the "typological" exegesis of certain contemporary scholars is on an entirely different level. See the collection of essays edited by Claus Westermann under the title *Probleme alttestamentlicher Hermeneutik* (1960).

32 *Akt und Sein*, p. 139.

33 Reprinted with the permission of the publisher from *Prisoner for God: Letters and Papers from Prison*, pp. 153-154, by Dietrich Bonhoeffer, tr. by Reginald Fuller. Copyright 1953 by The Macmillan Company. All other excerpts from *Prisoner for God* in this essay are used by permission.

34 *Ibid.*, p. 79.

35 *Ibid.*, pp. 121-125.

36 *Ibid.*, p. 124.

37 *Ibid.*, pp. 125-126.

38 The excellent lectures of Eberhard Bethge delivered at the Chicago Theological Seminary and published in the Seminary *Register* (Feb., 1961, pp. 1-38) shed much light on the meaning of the "secret discipline" to which Bonhoeffer calls the Church (see especially p. 35). I can not see, however, how the Church really "exposes itself in its very existence" to the world if it keeps its treasures safe from profanation in its inner, secret life as it lives in and for the world.

39 *Prisoner for God (op. cit.)*, p. 157.

40 *Ibid.*, pp. 163-164.

41 *Ibid.*, pp. 166-167.

42 *Ibid.*, p. 169.

43 On this point see the essay by Oskar Hammelsbeck in *Die Mündige Welt*, I (1955), 46-61, especially 57-61. See also the essay by Gerhard Ebeling in *Die Mündige Welt*, II (1956).

44 *Prisoner for God (op. cit.)*, p. 177.

45 *Ibid.*, pp. 178-181.

6

The Early Answer to the Question
Concerning Jesus Christ

In the winter and the summer of 1932 Bonhoeffer wrote a friend that
he himself was no longer sympathetic to his product Act and Being;
now the problem of the concretion of the Word in its proclamation
forced itself on him. His biblical studies, his international experiences,
his personal maturation, his concerns for a troubled Church led him to
this. As he became obsessed with this necessity he came to the clearer
understanding that "concreteness" was not at all a mere matter of ter-
minological adaptation; that it inhered in the "essential concreteness
of Christ" (Bethge). "The message is concrete in itself not because its
content is transcendence but because it is the incarnated, actualized in
the person next to me."

At the crucial turn in this work of exposition Bonhoeffer delivered
what seemed to him the most difficult lectures of his life, a series on
Christology, in 1933. In the four-volume collected works, no single
piece can compete for interest and importance with Bethge's recompo-
sition of these lectures from students' notes. Bethge sees them as a
summary in concrete terms of what lay before them in Bonhoeffer's
work. Another interpreter, John Godsey, suggests that they serve as a
summary and a prefiguration of later interests. (Perhaps someone will
take pains to translate these notes of 1933 for publication in booklet
form—they belong among Bonhoeffer's most important works.) Godsey,
who accents Christology so heavily in his interpretation, unfortunately
did not have this particular lecture sequence before him—otherwise he
could have made his point even more vividly.

Bonhoeffer chose to present his only concentrated study of his central
theological theme not in the format of biblical exegesis—at which he
was an extremely gifted amateur—but rather in his own discipline, systematic and historical theology. The logical choice for an interpreter to
bring the main themes of these lectures to an English-speaking audience

is Jaroslav Pelikan of Yale Divinity School, formerly of the University of Chicago. Few Americans have equipped themselves as he has done to understand the long tradition of dogmatic theology. The author of almost a dozen books in the field of historical theology, he is a more than competent guide into Bonhoeffer's main strands.

This is one of the most positive essays in the book. At the same time, Dr. Pelikan expresses some uneasiness concerning what remains a hazard in Bonhoeffer's thought, coming close as it does to a christomonistic pattern. If God is (as was said in Act and Being) somehow "haveable," graspable—then how does his own freedom protect itself from manipulation by men? Is this not the charter for mere immanentism or—as many misinterpreters of the late letters would have it—a direct and uncritical acceptance of the world? Is this not near the Ebionite heresy? Pelikan finds Bonhoeffer largely successfully defining himself over against these tendencies. Without careful attention to the Christology lectures of 1933 as a substructure for the last letters, there is danger that unthinking students may seriously mistreat his thought. Pelikan would agree with Harrelson: exegetically and methodologically Bonhoeffer by himself can hardly be this generation's guide—it is his comprehensiveness, directness, and theological intuition that makes him an important figure.

Bonhoeffer's *Christologie* of 1933

By Jaroslav Pelikan

ADOLF Harnack died on June 10, 1930. His long and almost incredibly productive career as a theological scholar had been devoted to the illumination and documentation of many problems in the history of the early Church, but no problem was more nearly central to his scholarly and theological concern than the doctrine of the person of Christ. The two works for which Harnack is best known even today, his *History of Dogma* and his lectures on *The Essence of Christianity*, both make this doctrine a predominant topic. In the former work, especially in its first volume, Harnack had traced the evolution of the Christian doctrine of the coequality of Christ with the Father. Then, in the second volume, he had shown how the orthodox doctrine of the Trinity had emerged from this doctrine. At the conclusion of his great work, in the third volume of the *Dogmengeschichte*, Harnack had asserted that the Reformation was the end of dogma, in theological principle if not in historical fact. Applying this assertion to the doctrine of the person of Christ, Harnack's *Das Wesen des Christentums* was an eloquent, if somewhat popularized, effort to state an understanding of Christ without a dogmatic Christology.[1]

Speaking for his generation of theological students, Dietrich Bonhoeffer gratefully accepted the scholarly legacy bequeathed by Adolf Harnack the theologian: "genuine freedom of research, of activity, and of life, and a profound [sense of] being sustained and grasped by the eternal ground of all thought and life." [2] Bonhoeffer's eulogy for Harnack and his other statements about the master make it clear that Bonhoeffer could not join the company of those whose quest for certainty has caused them to suppose that they have outgrown Adolf Harnack.[3] "That you were our teacher for many hours—this has passed away. But that we have the right to call ourselves your pupils—this abides," wrote Bonhoeffer to Harnack upon the latter's retirement in 1929.[4] Pupil of Harnack that he was, Bonhoeffer defended Rudolf Bultmann against the zeal without knowledge that dared to attack Bultmann's ideas about myth in the New Testament without ever having worked through Bultmann's commentary on the Fourth Gospel.[5] Thus Bonhoeffer knew that he stood in the succession of the historical and critical theology associated with the name of Adolf Harnack.

Yet less than two months after the death of Harnack, Bonhoeffer could declare, in his inaugural lecture at Harnack's Berlin, that the role of Christology in Luther's thought had been underestimated by most theologians, even by Karl Holl; and he could summarize his discussion of the problem of man in the language of a christological confession: "Christ exists among us as the Church, the Church [6] in the hiddenness of the historical. The Church is the hidden Christ among us. But therefore man is never alone, but exists only through the Church, which brings Christ to him, incorporates him into herself, and draws him into her life. Man in Christ is man in the Church; where he is, there the Church is." [7] Certainly a "high" doctrine of Christ and an even "higher" doctrine of the Church, to come from a pupil of Adolf Harnack about to become a Dozent in Harnack's own university!

Often a theologian's early writing contains, albeit only seminally, the major themes of his mature thought. So it was, for example, with The Incarnation of the Word of God by

Athanasius. The brief comments on the presence of Christ in the Church at the end of Bonhoeffer's inaugural lecture of 1930 were the germ for a complete course, of perhaps eighteen lectures, in the summer semester of 1933. Not until 1960, however, did these lectures become available to more than a select group. Eberhard Bethge, the editor of Bonhoeffer's collected works, has reconstructed the *Christologie* of 1933 from notes taken and preserved by several of those who heard the lectures.[8] Concerning this reconstruction and the circumstances under which the lectures were originally delivered Bethge writes: "This was a two-hour lecture course during the summer, in the midst of tumultuous events in the political life of the Church. Although Bonhoeffer did not allow his concentration to be diverted, he did assert that no series of lectures caused him more trouble than this one. It was his final regular academic work. For the editor its rediscovery is the high point of [this] third volume." [9] Although any such reconstruction of a man's words from notes taken by his hearers and students must be used with caution—as we have discovered in the case of Luther's exegetical lectures—the substantial authenticity of Bonhoeffer's *Christologie* is attested to both by the testimony of those who heard the lectures and by a comparison of the *Christologie* with other writings whose authenticity is incontestable.

The theme of Bonhoeffer's *Christologie* is the presence of Christ. He found it impossible, after the critical work of Harnack and other historical theologians, to make the traditional notion of the two natures in Christ the basis of his lectures. Nor could he, on the other hand, accept some conception or other of the historical Jesus and elevate this to the status of a new christological dogma. Instead he took his start from the "for me" in the language of the Reformers about Christ. "Christ for me" is a matter neither of dogma nor of literary-historical research into the Gospels, but of the Church's experience. This Christ is not merely remembered.

He is really present within and alongside the Church in her
battles, granting his good gifts and Spirit. Only when this real
presence of Christ is seen in the full scope of its power may a
Christology go on to a consideration of orthodoxy and heresy,
the dogma of the two natures, the problem of the Trinity, and
the other questions that have traditionally engaged the systematic theologians. And even when a Christology does reflect
upon these questions, the real presence of Jesus Christ makes
many of the traditional answers, and even some of the traditional questions, no longer possible.

To introduce and analyze the *Christologie* of 1933, this
essay will follow the main lines of Bonhoeffer's outline.[10] It will
not, however, attempt to condense an already succinct German
prose into even briefer theses. From time to time we shall be
quoting directly from the *Christologie*, and at other times we
shall be paraphrasing it. Bonhoeffer's lectures had to include
a large number of the traditional themes; for this was an
academic course, and a course in Christology, not a course in
the Christology of Dietrich Bonhoeffer. Our concern, on the
other hand, is with the Christology of Dietrich Bonhoeffer.
Hence we shall emphasize those features of the work that are
in some way distinctive, if not indeed unique, passing more
lightly over the conventional christological materials. Bonhoeffer's original outline envisioned three major divisions:

    I. The Present Christ
   II. The Historical Christ
  III. The Eternal Christ

But as it must do at one time or another to all lecturers, the
end of the course came upon Bonhoeffer before he had had an
opportunity to go into the third division at all. The lectures
appear, therefore, with only the first two of these divisions, to
which the two major sections of the present essay will correspond. We shall close with some critical and constructive
observations of our own.

The Real Presence as Mystery

Traditional christological orthodoxy has always faced the peril that the sublimity of its subject matter may beguile it into metaphysical speculation. The What of the real presence easily turns into a How, and orthodoxy is equated with a theoretical alchemy of the incarnation. In its justified revulsion from this distortion of the theological task, an evangelical theology of the Cross attempts to confine its attention to the saving deeds of Christ and to leave ontological questions behind. "To know Christ," said the Reformers, "is to know his blessings." [11] Understandable though this reaction is, it is finally an abdication of theology from its responsibility to speak of the real presence of Jesus Christ as a unity of *Act* and *Being*. That responsibility does indeed forbid Christology to ask the question How. But it obliges Christology to ask the question What and the question Where, for by the answers to these two questions the mystery of Jesus Christ is made clear in all its mysteriousness.

What is Jesus Christ? The *Christologie* gives a threefold answer: Word, Sacrament, Church. When the New Testament calls Christ the Word or Logos of God, it assigns him a special status in the being of God. But Christ as Word is God's address to man. The Word as idea can be passive and dormant, but the Word as address is possible only in a relationship; the Word as idea is a timeless truth, but the Word as address takes place in time and history. To the Word as idea one can be related as a knower or a speculator, but to the Word as address one is obliged to give some sort of response. Here Bonhoeffer, like other theologians of the Word, capitalizes upon a progression from *Wort* (word) to *Antwort* (response) to *Verantwortlichkeit* (responsibility). Like the related and equally untranslatable German distinction between *Gabe* (gift) and *Aufgabe* (task), this play on words enables a theology to speak of the connection between divine revelation and human response in a manner that does justice to them both. But Christ as the Word of God is the Christ of the real presence. He is present not only *in* the word of the Church, but also *as* the word of the Church, really and personally present in the proclamation, which is "the wealth and the poverty of the Church." Indeed, the proclamation of the Church is paradigmatic for the relation between the divine and the human in Christ. Christ is not half God and half man; nor is the proclamation partly the Word of God and partly the word of man. Rather, one must be able to point to this utterly human word and to say of it: "This is the Word of God." To do otherwise is to ask the wrong question and therefore to be doomed to get the wrong answer.

The necessity of asking the right question becomes even more evident in the definition of Christ as Sacrament. A false inquiry into the possibility of the sacramental presence led both Reformed and Lutheran theology into a labyrinth. Calvinism ended up positing a real presence of the Logos outside the man Jesus Christ (the *extra Calvinisticum*), thus undercutting the What of the real presence and reintroducing the question of the How. Lutheran theology, beginning with Luther himself, yielded to the temptation of asking the question How. The speculative distinction between several modes of the presence of Christ (*ubiquitas, multivolipraesentia*), which became a preoccupation of Orthodox Lutheran dogmatics, did identify the Logos with Jesus Christ, but only by positing a real presence of Jesus Christ outside the sphere of divine revelation! Such is the havoc wrought by the How. Yet it does not invalidate a eucharistic Christology. For the right eucharistic question is also the right christological question: "Who is present in the Sacrament?" And the answer must read: "Present is the entire person of the God-man in his exaltation and humiliation. . . . Christ exists in such a way that he is *existentialiter* present in the Sacrament. His sacramental being [*Sakrament-sein*] is not a special property, a

quality among others, but this is how he exists in the Church."
He who is both Creator and creature, both our Brother and
our Lord, crucified and risen and ascended—he it is who is
really present in the Sacrament. Nor is it enough to say that
he is represented in the Sacrament. For only one who is
absent can be, or needs to be, represented.

And Jesus Christ is not the absent one. His real presence in
the Sacrament cannot be dissociated from the real presence in
the Church. "The presence in Word and Sacrament is related
to the presence in the Church as reality is related to form. . . .
The Church between ascension and second coming is his
form, and the only one at that." Christ is the Church both as
Word and as Sacrament. As Word, he speaks in such a way as
to create the form of the Church, which thus becomes not
only the recipient of the Word of revelation but herself a
revelation and a Word of God. As Sacrament, Christ assumes
bodily form to be present, and the Church is his body. Therefore "the concept of the body, applied to the Church, is not
merely a functional concept, relevant only to the members
of this body; but in its comprehensiveness and centrality it is
a concept of him who is present, exalted and humbled." In
the authentic writings of Paul, Christ as the body is not
distinguished from Christ as the head. Only after Paul, in
Ephesians, does such a distinction arise. Yet Christ as the
body of the Church is still the Church's Lord. Thus the
theological answer to the question, "Who is Jesus Christ?"
must point to Word, Sacrament, and Church as the forms of
his real presence. But it also finds itself compelled to ask a
further question—if not the question of How, which has been
excluded by definition, then certainly the question of Where.

What is the locus of Jesus Christ? The structure of his
person requires some word about the structure of his existence
within time and space. Where is he, then? "He stands in my
stead there where I ought to stand and cannot. He stands on
the border of my existence, beyond my existence and yet for

me." From this it follows that I have been separated from the "I" I should be, and that I stand in judgment because of this separation. Christ is both the rediscovery of the authentic center of my human existence and the border of that existence, a border that can be known only from beyond. The centrality of the person of Jesus Christ belongs to the definition of his person. He is the Mediator; and as the question of What yielded a threefold answer, so the question of Where also requires three distinct but not separate answers. The locus of Jesus Christ is: his real presence at the center of human existence; his real presence at the center of history; his real presence at the center of nature. And in each of these the phrase "at the center" could also become "as the center."

If Christ stands at the center of our human existence, this must not be understood to mean what the idealism of the nineteenth century meant by such an expression: that the human personality, as the highest expression of the thought and feeling of man, is also the point of contact with God as ultimate Personality. Perhaps an English coinage like "personhood," as distinguished from "personality," can best convey this distinction. When Christ is seen as occupying the center of human existence, this means also that he is the one who has fulfilled the law of human existence, which man has been both unable and unwilling to keep. Thus he stands as a judgment upon man for his failure to meet the demands of this law. And he is a judgment even as he is the bringer of a new righteousness and a divine justification into the center of human existence. That is why it is not legitimate to reason from human existence or human personality to the personality of Christ as the center of human existence, but only vice versa; for Christ is "man's boundary and his judgment, but also the beginning of his new existence and its center."

As the philosophical effort to interpret Christ as the center of human existence shatters on the biblical picture both of Christ and of human existence, so the apologetic attempt to find historical evidence for the biblical claim that Christ was sent only "when the fulness of the time was come" (Galatians 4:4) is both impossible and useless. After all, "comparison with relative entities and proofs of a relative question do not issue in an absolute." Here, too, theology must be careful to raise the right question, and that is not the question of absoluteness. So it will not do to set the historism of the nineteenth century in opposition to its personalistic idealism, as though a preoccupation with Christ as the center of history could produce an objectivity that is absent from the interpretation of Christ as the center of human existence. It is no more possible to move from the study of history to Christ than it is to pass from human personality to Christ. Only on the basis of the real presence of Jesus Christ does it become evident what the quests and the longings of human history have meant. These are not self-illuminating or self-explanatory; but as the center of history, Christ makes sense of them also.

Viewed from this center, history is seen as the universal expectation of a Messiah. Even where no Christ is expected, in Reinhold Niebuhr's phrase, there remains an awareness that history must have a meaning and an expectation that history itself will produce such a meaning. History "bears within itself the promise of becoming filled with God, the womb for the birth of God." Only in Israel is the profound sense of this meaning and promise to be found, for it was given to the prophets of Israel to see that the Messiah cannot provide the meaning of history in some immanent and self-evident fashion, but can become the center of history only through the free and mysterious action of the sovereign God. Elsewhere the expectation of a center of history condemns itself to bitterness and disappointment. When Christ does come as the center of history, therefore, he is simultaneously the fulfillment and the destruction of all human expectations and hopes: "the destruction, in that the visible Messiah fails to come and the fulfillment is hidden as it happens; the fulfillment, in that God has truly entered into history and the expected one is now truly there." Or to put it in traditional Christian language, the search for the center of human history ends at the Cross of the humiliated Christ.

The Christ who stands at the center of history is the Christ of Word, Sacrament, and Church. Hence the Church, as the form of his real presence between his resurrection and his second coming, is likewise the center of history, namely, of that history which is made by the state. It is the function and essence of the state to enable a nation to move toward the fulfillment of its destiny. This the state does by the maintenance of law and order. Within this state the Church stands as the center, not empirically or visibly, but with the hiddenness of the real presence. "In its hiddenness [the Church] is the meaning and the promise of the state, judging and justifying [the state] in its essence." As Christ is both the center and the boundary, so the Church acts not only as the center of that history which is made by the state, but as its boundary as well. This does not mean that the Church establishes some new law, as though Christ had come as a new Moses. But it does mean that the Church proclaims an action of God by which the state is both fulfilled and transcended. The Cross has renewed the state as well as the Church, shattering and fulfilling and affirming the "secular order."

In this sense the real presence of Christ at the center of history takes a dual form. Christ is present both as Church and as state, both only for those who receive him as Word, Sacrament, and Church. The reign of Christ has been divided into Church and state, what Luther called "the two realms [Regimente]," the realm of the right hand (Church) and the realm of the left hand (state). Whether the state knows it or not, it draws its life from the Christ who is the center of all history, whose real presence is known and available to his Church. "As the center of history, Christ is the Mediator between God and the state, [and is so] in the form of the

Church. As the center of history, he is likewise the Mediator between God and this Church. For he is also the center of this Church, which can be the center of history only for that reason."

The third locus of Jesus Christ, in addition to human existence and history, is nature: Christ is the center and the Mediator between God and the world of nature. In the original plan of creation, nature was meant to be a Word of God, but the guilt of man has enslaved it. Now mute and fallen, nature cannot live up to its destiny or find its freedom. Unlike human existence and history, it does not need reconciliation; rather, it needs liberation, as it demonstrates when it asserts its brute force over man. The "catastrophes" of nature are a hidden expression of nature's yearning for the new creation in Christ. When the Church proclaims the redemption accomplished in Christ, it announces his redemptive presence, even though he is still hidden. The sign of this real presence at the center of nature is that "in the Sacraments, elements of the old creation have become elements of the new creation," speaking for a muted nature and proclaiming to the believers the creative Word of God. Although Protestant theology has traditionally concerned itself with the implications of the real presence of Jesus Christ for the interpretation both of human existence and of history, it has not spoken very much about its implications for nature. Yet existence, history, and nature are finally inseparable. For "in fact, human nature is always history and always nature. As the fulfiller of the law and the liberator of the creation, the Mediator performs these acts for all of human existence. He is exactly the same one, as the intercessor 'for me,' the end of the old world, and the beginning of the new world of God."

The Real Presence as Dogma

The mystery of the real presence of Jesus Christ is the mystery of the Who and the Where, and it dare not be dis-

torted into the mystery of the How. But is not the christological dogma, as expounded by orthodoxy and as exposed by
Harnack, a grandiose theory of the How of the real presence?
And must not the methodological chastity of historical research into the life of Jesus be kept unspotted by the covert
metaphysics of a dogmatic Christology?

Only if dogmatic Christology and historical research remain
together can true methodological chastity be preserved; only
the christological dogma can defend the Church's witness
to the real presence against the various false answers to the
false question of the How. For of itself, historical research
cannot produce answers to the questions that theology puts to
it. Christian dogmatics is impossible without a certainty about
the historicity of Jesus Christ, and in the era of liberal theology
historical research was asked to produce and support such
certainty. But "historical research can never negate absolutely,
because it can never affirm absolutely. . . . Absolute certainty
about a historical fact is eo ipso unattainable." For the dogma
of the Church, therefore, the foundation dare not be the
history of Jesus Christ as past, but the presence of Jesus Christ
as history. His attestation of himself, in the power of his
resurrection, provides this foundation. The miracle of his
real presence in the Church substantiates what historical
research can neither negate absolutely nor affirm absolutely,
and it does so through the Scriptures.

Thus the real presence of the resurrected Christ forms the
only tenable presupposition for theological method. The
historical research of theological liberalism did not produce a
valid method, but neither did the theological absolutism of
orthodoxy. For "verbal inspiration is a poor substitute for the
resurrection. It represents the denial of the unique [alleinig]
presence of the Risen One. It eternalizes history, instead of
viewing and acknowledging history on the basis of the eternity
of God." To repossess the christological dogma today, we must
not attempt to go around the historical and critical insights of

liberal theology, even though we can and must go through this theology. Indeed, in our day the scope and the meaning of the christological dogma have become clearer. It was the function of dogma, as prescribed by the councils, to set the limits for theological thought, while the exegesis and speculation of the Church's theologians, working within these limits, investigated the positive content of Christology. In short, one of the most important tasks of any Christology is the definition of heresy; only after such a definition can theology be free to pursue its authentic vocation.

The heresy of Docetism, whether in its ancient or in its modern form, seeks to explain the real presence of Jesus Christ by means of some distinction between the eternal idea of Christ and its temporal manifestation in Jesus. "The idea is substance, the manifestation is accident. Christ the God is substance, Jesus the man is accident." In its earliest form, the Docetic heresy shaped the Christology of the Gnostics, to whom the real presence of Christ as Jesus was a matter of indifference. All that really mattered was the divine idea, the absolute and impassable God, who had to be screened away from the flux of creation. When the christological dogma of the early Church rejected Gnostic Docetism in the name of the real presence, it failed to see that this notion of God was at least partly at fault; therefore orthodox Christology retained, in the fluctuation between *anhypostasia* and *enhypostasia*, a vestigial remnant of the very heresy it condemned. Despite the dedication of modern Protestant liberalism to the true humanity of Jesus, its Christology is still Docetic; for, like Gnosticism, it is interested primarily in the idea. This idea may be human personality or value or truth, and Jesus is interpreted as the representative or the bearer of the idea. So the real presence of God in the history of Jesus Christ melts into the historical process. Hence "the Church must reject every form of Docetism . . . [and] with it every form of Greek idealistic thought, insofar as this operates with the distinction between idea and manifestation. Idealism undermines the fundamental proposition of all theology, that God, by free grace, has become a real man."

Docetism is a characteristically Greek heresy, but the Ebionite heresy has its roots in Israelite thought. It seeks to explain the mystery of the incarnation and the real presence by insisting upon the concreteness of the historical figure Jesus Christ. He is not the metamorphosis of the divine into human form, for this would be blasphemy. He is, rather, the adopted Son of God, upon whom the Spirit of God descended at baptism. Jesus is not God by nature, but he "becomes God" as he subjects his will more and more to the will of God. Clearly superior to Docetism in many ways, this adoptionism "keeps in view the concrete Jesus, the real man. Salvation is tied not to an ideal picture, but to the [Suffering] Servant. At the same time, Ebionitism keeps God the Creator in view also." But it is so impressed by the transcendence of God and by the creatureliness of man that it cannot bring the Creator and the creature together even in the person of Christ. Yet the salvation wrought by Christ is impossible unless there is a real presence of the Creator in this creature. Despite its superiority to Docetism, Ebionite adoptionism cannot be the Church's Christology either; for the Church's Christology must reject any effort that safeguards either the full humanity or the full divinity of Jesus Christ without asserting both. "The two How questions of the Docetic and the Ebionite Christology must both yield to the question of Who."

Not in the conflict between these two early heresies, however, but in the christological controversies of the fifth century did the orthodox dogma of the person of Christ come to maturity. The Council of Chalcedon in 451 directed its formula against both the Nestorian and the Monophysite heresy, ruling out any attempt "to speak of divinity and humanity in Christ as objects [dinglich] and to distinguish between them as things." It was the greatness of this Chalcedonian formula that it spoke negatively. From both the heresies it was attacking it borrowed the terminology with which it prescribed the tension proper to Christology even as it described the boundaries of christological orthodoxy. If anything, subsequent theological history has confirmed the validity of Chalcedon. Both the Lutheran and the Reformed dogmaticians of the sixteenth and seventeenth centuries used the terminology of Chalcedon and sought to articulate their Christologies within the Chalcedonian boundaries; but Lutheranism continually skirted the edge of the Eutychian heresy proscribed by Chalcedon, while Reformed Christology ran the danger of separating the divine and the human in Christ after the fashion of Nestorianism.

As in the ancient Church the most elaborate christological development took place where Christology was "highest"— that is, in Alexandrian theology—so it was in Lutheranism rather than in Calvinism that the most imposing speculative structure was erected on the foundations of the christological dogma. Neither Calvinism nor Lutheranism recognized how radically Chalcedon had broken with the entire question of How. The result of Chalcedon is this: "By its negative insistence upon contradictions, it transcended the doctrine of the two natures and really says that the matter of Jesus Christ cannot be grasped and resolved into a unity by means of the concept 'nature.' This critical sense of Chalcedon must be carried further."

The implications of this analysis of christological heresy for the positive task of interpreting the real presence of Jesus Christ today may be summarized in three propositions:

- A unilinear declaration about Jesus Christ is illegitimate.
- It is invalid to speak of the divinity and the humanity of Jesus Christ as objects (*dinglich*).
- The question of How raises problems with which it cannot cope, and therefore it itself leads to the question of Who.

On the basis of these three propositions, which set the ground rules for theology, the individual theologian has the right and the duty to reflect on the picture of Christ given in the New Testament. At least two themes emerge from such reflection and form the positive content of the dogma of the real presence: Jesus Christ as the Incarnate One; Jesus Christ as the Humiliated and the Exalted One.

To give "Jesus Christ the Incarnate One" as a theme of positive Christology is to subject the doctrine of the incarnation to the third of these propositions, replacing How with Who. The question of How is at work in the effort to explain the Who by means of the virgin birth, for the first answer to the question Who is: "Jesus was man just as I am. Of him alone is it truly valid to say [with Terence] that nothing human was alien to him." This authentically human Jesus is the subject of the confessional sentence: "He is God for us." Not some prior definition of the being of God, based upon reason or experience, but the concreteness of the Incarnate One is the concern of faith. "If Jesus Christ is to be described as God, it will not do to speak of the divine essence, of his omnipotence or of his omniscience; but we must speak of this weak man among sinners, of his manger and of his Cross. . . . In Christology one looks at the entire historical man Jesus and declares about him that he is God." Both the story of the birth of Jesus, which Docetism can interpret in a way that makes him less than true man, and the story of the baptism of Jesus, which Ebionitism can interpret in a way that makes him less than true God, apply to one and the same person. In him the Creator is really present, in him the creature attains to glory. But the glorification of God in his creature happens under the veil of the Cross.

Therefore a positive Christology must speak not alone of the Incarnate One, but also of the Humiliated and the Exalted One. If incarnation is identified with humiliation, exaltation can be interpreted as the return of Christ from humanity to the eternal life of the Trinity. Then the whole point of Christology is lost, for both humiliation and exaltation must be predicated of one and the same Incarnate One. He was humiliated in that he took upon himself "the likeness of sinful flesh" (Romans 8:3); he was incarnate in relation to the original creation, but humbled in relation to the fallen creation. So completely did he take upon himself the very form of human existence that he became "the worst sinner of all," as Luther says. The New Testament does not describe him as a sinless phantom; nor is his temptation a puppet show, but a genuine conflict. Only as the one who passed through conflict and sin does he emerge as "the sinless One, the holy One, the eternal One, the Lord, and the Son of the Father." Thus there always remains the possibility of our being offended at him. Even at his exaltation we can take offense, for the form of that exaltation is the resurrection and the story of the empty grave. This story does not rescue Christian faith from the ambiguity of the historical, but accentuates that ambiguity; "even as the Risen One he does not abolish his incognito."

The Church lives by the power of his humiliation and exaltation. Daily it re-enacts God's gift in Christ, receiving the forgiveness of sins through the real presence of the Incarnate, Humiliated, and Exalted One, in whom God enables faith to see the meaning and the promise of life.

And here the lectures ended. At least some of their power, as well as the power of the lecturer, should have become evident by now from the preceding summary. Dietrich Bonhoeffer was a theologian who was not ashamed to think and speak theologically. In his method he combined perspectives and motifs that most other theologians have set into disjunction: loyalty to tradition did not close him to the historical-critical method; Protestantism did not obscure the centrality of the doctrine of the Church in Christology; Lutheranism did not blind him to the dangers of a eucharistic Christology; ethical concern did not cause him to look for dogmatic short cuts. As the other essays in this volume show, Bonhoeffer did many things exceptionally well. It may seem a cavil to ask whether there was anything theological that he did superbly. Specifically, a study of the *Christologie* of 1933 evokes many questions about the long-term adequacy of Bonhoeffer's christological method. Of these questions we list three:

• Is this interpretation of heresy and of dogma an accurate report of the history of Christology? There is no avoiding the impression that Bonhoeffer's formulation of the central issues—How versus Who—has caused him to draw both the contrasts and the affinities in that history according to an *a priori* pattern. To cite only the most obvious instance, even the rhetoric of the *Christologie* is probably insufficient to persuade most readers that the historical-critical liberalism of the nineteenth century was guilty chiefly of the Docetic heresy. When Bonhoeffer connects liberalism to Gnosticism in this way, he expresses a useful insight and scores a debating point. But it is the type of insight one would expect from an exceptionally bright student rather than from a well-trained, though immature, scholar. Although Bonhoeffer could have drawn upon the historical research not only of Harnack but of Harnack's pupils and critics, the materials of history of dogma in these lectures do not rise much above the level of the textbook or theological encyclopedia.

• Does this conception of Christology do justice to the full range of biblical language and imagery about Jesus Christ? Perhaps the most surprising characteristic of this *Christologie* is the relative paucity of references to the Scriptures. This means not only that there are not very many individual passages cited or expounded, but also that they are often the most obvious ones, and that even these are not exploited for their fuller or more subtle meanings. In 1933 the study of the New

Testament had come to the end of the road "from Reimarus to Wrede" and was only beginning to move out of that impasse. The second edition of Martin Dibelius' *Formgeschichte des Evangeliums* appeared in that very year, and the second edition of Rudolf Bultmann's *Geschichte der synoptischen Tradition* had come out two years earlier. Although there are echoes of these works in Bonhoeffer's insistence that the Jesus of history cannot be separated from the Christ of the Church's faith, he does not capitalize upon the exciting christological possibilities already available to him. Karl Heim, Lionel Thornton, and Karl Adam are all contemporaries of his who penetrated with more imagination into the christological implication of the new exegesis of the New Testament.

• Does this restatement of the Church's dogma speak to the spirit of the time both where it wants to hear and where it needs to hear the Word of God? A theology must look for the place where men expect to hear, and it must find the place where men need to hear. Even by the 1930's, did the *Zeitgeist* need to be disabused of idealism, or had it already lost itself so completely in its immanence that anything "beyond" seemed an illusion? In the Alexandria of the fifth century, or for that matter the Wittenberg of the seventeenth, it was necessary to warn intellectuals against a preoccupation with essence at the expense of existence. But in the Berlin of the 1930's, or for that matter the New York of the 1960's, a philosophy of existence has hemmed the *Zeitgeist* into so tight a box of the *hic et nunc* that not even history and tradition, much less the world of essences and ideas, can become real for the intelligentsia. To Rudolf Bultmann one must put the question: Does the contemporary mind need the help of theologians to learn that the message of the Gospel is self-understanding, and is American evangelical Protestantism so lost in objectivism that it needs to recover a vision of the self? Thus also one must raise a question about Dietrich Bonhoeffer's preoccupation with the concreteness of Jesus Christ:

Is it symptomatic that he barely extricates himself from the Ebionite heresy?

Christology is always both *Gabe* and *Aufgabe*. It is *Gabe* because Christ himself is a gift, the gift of God *pro nobis*. It is *Aufgabe* because it must take the legacy of Scripture and tradition about Christ and seek to make sense of it again. No Christology is ever a finished product, and no generation can simply appropriate the Christology of its predecessors. The publication of Bonhoeffer's *Christologie* and of this volume will have done a disservice to the present generation if terms like "concreteness" or "anti-Docetic" or "Who, not How" establish themselves with the same tenacity that has attended "static versus dynamic" or "knowledge of, not knowledge about" in the past two or three decades. The Protestant theology of the United States needs a period of fresh new exegesis, not merely of crypto-systematic "biblical theology," if it is to learn to speak christologically again. From the fathers, creeds, and councils American Protestantism must regain the Catholic substance it has inherited in such meagerness and spent with such profligacy. Bonhoeffer can help us to see the problems and the resources. More than this he cannot do—but neither can any other theologian.

Notes for Essay 6

1 On the contemporary significance of Harnack's work, see Rudolf Bultmann, "Introduction" to Adolf Harnack, *The Essence of Christianity* (New York: Harper & Brothers, 1957); also Wilhelm Pauck, *The Heritage of the Reformation*, 2nd ed. (Boston: Beacon Press, 1961).

2 Dietrich Bonhoeffer, "*Rede zum Gedächtnis Adolf von Harnacks am 15. Juni 1930 in der Kaiser-Wilhelm-Gesellschaft*," *Gesammelte Schriften* (henceforth abbreviated as *G. S.*), III, 61.

3 Cf. Jaroslav Pelikan, "Introduction" to Adolf Harnack, *The Mission and Expansion of Christianity in the First Three Centuries* (New York: Harper & Brothers, 1962).

4 Bonhoeffer to Harnack, Dec. 18, 1929, *G. S.*, III, 19.

5 Bonhoeffer to Ernst Wolf, March 24, 1942, *G. S.*, III, 45-46.

6 "*Christus existiert unter uns als Gemeinde, als Kirche. . . .*" Neither "congregation" nor "community" renders *Gemeinde* adequately, for it has (or has acquired) in German some of the connotations of the English word "Church" that *Kirche* does not have. Therefore I have finally decided to render *Gemeinde* with "Church."

7 On Christology in Luther, "*Die Frage nach dem Menschen in der gegenwärtigen Philosophie und Theologie*" (July 31, 1930), *G. S.*, III, 76; the quotation in the text, *ibid.*, 83-84.

8 *Christologie*, *ibid.*, 166-242.

9 Eberhard Bethge, "Vorwort," *ibid.*, p. 9.

10 The subheads in my essay are my own, but they seem to me to reproduce Bonhoeffer's meaning. I have not given page references for each of the direct quotations, for they follow in sequence; the translations are my own throughout.

11 The quotation is from the 1521 edition of the *Loci communes* of Melanchthon.

7

The Christian in the Church Responding to the Answer in Jesus Christ

The last letters of Bonhoeffer were written so near the end that he was not able to detail all the implications of the new world-oriented Christian vision he held. Particularly, he did not find opportunity to depict forms of church life and, most of all, the character of worship in the emergent Church. This has led many superficially to abandon the disciplined devotional life in the name of religionless Christianity. When this is done, it is clear that Bonhoeffer's own experience of nurture and sustenance in prison must go unnoticed. Despite the temptations, the agonies, and the attractiveness of his potential future life "out in the world," he remained close to Sacrament and preached word, to the hymns of Paul Gerhardt, the Psalms, the music of Hugo Distler, and even some pietistic Christian norms.

Reginald Fuller in this essay on Liturgy and Devotion suggests that it is difficult to tie together Bonhoeffer's thoughts in Life Together with those in the last letters. Fuller is correct. In a way, they are not to be tied together, but to be seen in polarities, or in a dialectical relationship. The Church inhales and exhales; it engages in strategic retreat in order to advance; it ministers in the cave of refuge so that it can minister in the tent of the people of God on the march. The world-oriented Church presupposed the secret disciplines of ethics and devotion, oriented to a concrete fellowship of men and to the revelation of God in Jesus Christ.

Thus Bonhoeffer could describe his interest in liturgical and devotional discipline and retreat as "concentration for the outside." Under the cross of suspicion and secrecy he ministered to a fellowship of seminarians in order that he and they might spring forth to the day's tasks—sorrows and joys. Under the cross of imprisonment he ministered to a fellowship of prisoners so that he and they might accept the day and look forward to a wholly exposed and "worldly" future. Some people prefer the Bonhoeffer of the middle period, in the apparent luxury

167

of his conventicles, cells, secret seminaries, liturgical concerns; Eberhard Bethge calls this properly a transfer from "the bellicose ghetto" of Bonhoeffer to a "self-contained one." Others, in the interest of worldly immediacy forget the disciplines of this middle, devotional period. Each is a partial vision; here is where the double rhythms of the Christian life must be made apparent.

Reginald Fuller was assigned several tasks: to suggest this polarity; to relate Bonhoeffer to classic Christian norms of devotion; to see him in the light of the then-nascent Liturgical Movement; to introduce some of his continental modes of thinking on devotion to an Anglo-Saxon (in Fuller's case, Anglican) way. Fuller, a professor at Seabury-Western Theological Seminary near Chicago, has full right to be seen as an authoritative interpreter. The interests in the concrete aspects of preaching and liturgy are apparent in his numerous books, among them, What Is Liturgical Preaching? Every Bonhoeffer student in America will, further, recognize him as the translator of The Cost of Discipleship and Letters and Papers from Prison (Prisoner for God) and thus as one of the men who introduced Bonhoeffer to this continent.

Liturgy and Devotion

By Reginald H. Fuller

To associate Bonhoeffer with liturgy and devotion must seem
to many paradoxical, if not absurd. How could this prophet of
a religionless Christianity have cared for such esoteric pursuits?
Partly, that reaction would be because they do not know
Bonhoeffer. Of that, more later. But partly too it would be
because they do not know what liturgy and devotion really
are. Such people are hardly to be blamed. For liturgical enthusiasts like our high church seminarians, these matters are all
too often an esoteric hobby, antiquarian and esthetic. It is
such fun to debate the cut of a chasuble, the color of a stole,
or the cadence of a Gregorian chant! Bonhoeffer, like Gallio,
cared for none of these things. Yet, even here, one is bound
to insert a qualification. He *did* have a deep appreciation of
church music. He could become enthusiastic not, as it happens,
over plainsong, but about the Advent melody *Nun Komm der
Heiden Heiland*.[1] Yet it is the theological attitude, the "advent
situation" of expectancy, which the authentic form of the
melody expresses that really engages him. Nor was he insensi-
tive to the esthetic appeal of ceremonial:

> If you manage to get to Rome during Holy Week, do
> try and get to the service at St. Peter's on Maundy Thurs-
> day afternoon (it lasts roughly from two to six). It is
> really the service for Good Friday since the Roman
> Church anticipates its feasts from noon on the day be-

169

fore.[2] . . . On Maundy Thursday all the twelve candles on the altar are put out as a symbol of the flight of the disciples until at last there is only one candle left burning in the middle (for Christ). After that comes the washing of the altar. Early on Easter Eve, shortly before 7 a.m., there is the blessing of the font (I have a vague memory that it is connected with the ordination of young priests). Then at 12 noon the great Easter Alleluia is sung, the organ peals forth again, the mass bells ring, and the pictures are unveiled.[3]

All this, however, remains a peripheral and quite healthy interest which forms a legitimate place in any Christian's life. It is not mawkish or all-absorbing, as it was for the "Berneucheners" whom Bonhoeffer criticizes.

There is also dry-as-dust antiquarian liturgical scholarship, the sort that argues about the wording of the *epiklesis* or the position of the *Gloria in Excelsis* in the Mass. There is nothing of the kind in Bonhoeffer. Theology for him is essentially related to life: it and none of its branches are matters of mere academic, scholarly pursuits. His criticism of the Confessing Church for lapsing into "conservative restoration" hits just this kind of dry-as-dust liturgiology too:

> The important thing about that Church (i.e., the Confessing Church) is that it carries on the great concept of Christian theology, but that is all that it seems to do. There are, certainly, in these concepts the elements of genuine prophetic quality . . . and of genuine worship, and to that extent the message of the Confessing Church meets only with attention, hearing and rejection. But they remain unexplained and remote, because there is no interpretation of them.[4]

This criticism applies, *mutatis mutandis*, to what has passed for scholarly study of liturgy in the past.

For many again liturgy means, as it meant both to the Puritans and to seventeenth-century Anglican Caroline divines, fixed prayers read out of a book *versus* free, charismatic, *ex tempore* prayer. In that sense Bonhoeffer belonged to a liturgical church just as much as those who like the present writer have been brought up on the Book of Common Prayer. Every German Lutheran pastor carries his *Agenda* under the sleeve of his *Thalar* as he enters or leaves the church. He needs it for the liturgy of openings and closings of worship, in which the prayers from the book provide the bread for the "sermon sandwich," in which it is the *Wurst* of the word that we are really after. Behind this reduction of liturgy to a preface and postlude to the sermon lies distortion of liturgy into things said rather than things done. This distortion was both medieval and postmedieval, the only difference being that whereas the Old Priest "said Mass" and so offered the holy sacrifice for the people, the New Presbyter said the words of institution and so provided communion for the people. Was Bonhoeffer aware of this distortion of liturgy into something said by a sacerdotal figure for a dumb laity? There is nothing in his writings, so far as the present writer has discovered, to suggest that he would have thought of it in just this way. But wait a bit . . . to understand Bonhoeffer on liturgy we must step aside first and look at recent liturgical questions.

Liturgy, in essence, is neither an esthetic worship experience (a terrible expression which should be expurged from American Protestant vocabulary forthwith), nor is it an antiquarian science, nor is it prayers read out of a book. One of the great factors which transcends many barriers within the divided body of Christ is the liturgical movement. Taught by sound scholarship,[5] it has come to see that liturgy is basically the church's obedient response to the New Testament command, "Do this in remembrance of me." "Do" is in the plural: it is the action of a plurality of persons altogether, not of (say) a sacerdotal minister for a dumb laity, whether what he does is thought of in terms of offering sacrifice or providing the opportunities for individual communion. It is the action of a whole body of persons together, the action of the gathered church. "Do"—it is action. We do not go just to listen or to receive, but to *do* something. Pelagian? Not if it is *obedient response.* And if we are looking for grace without that obedient response, perhaps what we are looking for is "cheap grace," for it may be costly to have to forgo the luxury of my own private devotions and to muck in and *do* something with all sorts of other people. "Do *this.*" What? This—what the Lord himself did *and all of it:* not just "Receive," but the (seven) acts he did:

1. He took the bread.
2. He gave thanks.
3. He broke the bread.
4. He gave and they received it.

5. He took the cup.
6. He gave thanks.
7. He gave and they drank of it.

Very soon these seven acts were reduced to four by the combination of the bread and cup, so we get the four parts of the liturgy:

1. Offertory (taking of the elements)
2. Consecration (thanksgiving)
3. Fraction (breaking of the bread)
4. Communion

The doing of this is essentially liturgy. Liturgy has not necessarily anything to do with an esthetic ceremonial staged to create a religious atmosphere for a successful worship experience. Liturgy has not necessarily anything to do with reading prayers out of a book (the early Christians did not for some two hundred years). But it does mean doing these things, and doing them as a corporate body, each member playing his own part in the doing of it.

But this doing has a purpose and a meaning: "Do this in *remembrance of me.*" Not, so biblical scholars tells us, in order to think back to a person who lived or an event which happened in the dim and distant past. The purpose of the liturgical action is in order that in and through it God, according to his promise, may make the redemptive event of Christ present for our participation, in anticipation of its ultimate fulfillment in the *parousia*. This has several implications for our traditional theological positions. First, Catholics (Roman and Anglo-) ought to give up speaking of the Mass as a sacrifice which the priest or even the church *offers*. Carefully explained, this is a tenable statement, in the sense that the church as Christ's body is caught up into his sacrifice, but it needs such careful theological qualification that it is best avoided. The Mass is certainly something which the church *does* (here the Catholics are right), but the important thing about it is what in and through that action God does—which is to make the sacrifice of his Son present. Second, right-wing Protestants (Lutherans, moderate Anglicans, and high Calvinists) must give up thinking of the Holy Communion exclusively in terms of the individual reception of the Body and Blood of Christ. We must think of the Eucharist in terms of Real Action rather than of Real Presence—the real action of the church in and through which according to his promise the real act of God takes place. Left-wing Protestants must give up thinking of the Lord's Supper as a kind of Oberammergau passion play. The broken bread and the poured-out wine are not mere miming of the passion. In the liturgy the real actor is God, or more strictly speaking, God in Christ, God in Christ in his risen body. The liturgy is itself an integral part of the redemptive act, its bringing out of the past into the present.

And what of the effects of the liturgy? It is not simply that the individual receives grace and help to live the Christian life, not simply individual forgiveness of sins, not simply the individual "making his communion." The effect of the communion in Pauline terms is to cement the unity of the body of Christ:

> The bread which we break, is it not a participation in
> the body of Christ? Because there is one loaf, we who are
> many are one body, for we all partake of the same loaf
> (I Corinthians 10:17).

The liturgical movement is not concerned merely with the
doing of the liturgy within the four walls of the church building. It sees the liturgy as the mainspring of evangelism. We
traditionally think of evangelism as something done by individuals; whether it be the gifted evangelist in the crowded revival meeting, or the ordinary individual Christian witnessing
to the faith that is in him. The liturgical movement teaches us
to think of the church—the local liturgical community—as the
real instrument of evangelism. The church, by being the
church in the liturgy ("being the church" rather than "going
to church" is a slogan of the liturgical movement) exhibits
forth what the gospel really means: the mighty act of God in
Christ by which sinful, fragmented humanity is integrated
into the body of Christ and the fellowship of the Spirit. The
outsider, seeing in the liturgy what the church is and therefore
what the gospel is, is confronted with the challenge to decision. Paul again saw the evangelistic possibilities of liturgy:

> If therefore the whole church assembles . . . and an
> outsider or unbeliever enters . . . he will worship God
> and declare that God is really among you (I Corinthians
> 14:23-25).

Lastly, liturgy is intimately connected with the church's social task. Those who partake of the one bread and are ce-
mented into the one body go out into the world, and what if
they return to a world in which they are divided by race and
class? They are surely eating the bread and drinking the wine
to their own condemnation and are guilty of the body and
blood of Christ, if they sit down complacently and acquiesce
in the injustices which deny what they are, one body, one
humanity reintegrated in a common Head.

The communion is social dynamite, if we take really seriously the pattern of community known at the altar. The Church discovered that, in time, in the case of slavery. We have to discover it in terms of race and class and all that is involved for the distribution of the world's resources in the practice, in which we indulge so thoughtlessly each Sunday, of the absolute unconditional sharing of bread.[6]

Now Bonhoeffer was a little too early to have felt the full impact of the liturgical movement. There were, it is true, liturgical stirrings within German Lutheranism in the thirties, but they were mainly of the esthetic or the antiquarian type, and in the German church struggle the serious-minded were looking elsewhere for their inspiration—to the dialectical theology of Karl Barth. We must not therefore expect to find much of these particular insights in Bonhoeffer. At the same time there are certain parallels. Bonhoeffer has some conception of the objectivity of liturgy. He knows that worship is not just something instituted by a company of individuals getting together, but a stream of adoration that rises to heaven even in our absence. Indeed, he has something to tell us from prison about that important but neglected art, the art of being absent from church:

When I heard the church bells ringing this morning, I felt how I should have loved to go to church, but instead I followed St. John's example on the isle of Patmos, and held a nice little service of my own. I hardly felt lonely at all, for I was quite sure you were with me, and so were all the congregations with whom I have kept Whitsun in previous years.[7]

When we turn to *Life Together*, the little book in which Bonhoeffer speaks most directly of liturgical life, we are perhaps a little disappointed to find that the Holy Communion comes in almost as an afterthought at the end of the book, as if it were only a very occasional activity, rather than the center and focal point of the fellowship. We must of course remember the context out of which Life Together was written. It sprang from Bonhoeffer's experiences when he was in charge of the illegal pastors' seminary at Finkenwalde. Now to Anglicans it is almost unthinkable that in a community like a theological college or seminary the celebration of the Holy Communion should not be a frequent, if not daily, event in its life. I remember my surprise that this was not so in the Evangelisches Stift at Tübingen in 1938-1939, and I got the very significant explanation that the Lord's Supper was not an occasion for a group like a seminary but for the parochial congregation. There is a valid point here. The normal manifestation of the church is the local congregation: a seminary is not a congregation, but a highly specialized group within it. Since the Eucharist is essentially an activity of the whole church in one place, it could be questioned whether the specialized group ought to celebrate the Eucharist. At least a right understanding of the liturgy should preclude its doing so on a Sunday.[8]

Now it may well be that Bonhoeffer's comparative silence on the Lord's Supper within the common life of his seminary community is due to precisely this insight. If so, then he realized, as the liturgical movement does, that the Eucharist is essentially the act of the church, not of a specialized group of individuals within it. Quite possibly therefore the situation envisaged at the end of Life Together is that of the seminary community going together to the local parish church for the Sunday communion. In that case, since the ordering of the Lord's Supper is something which falls outside the regular activities of the seminary community, it does not call for direct consideration. The only concern within the seminary is that the group should prepare for it properly beforehand. Outlining the method of preparation Bonhoeffer speaks thus: "reconciled to God and man, Christians desire to receive the body and

blood of Jesus . . . the reception of the Lord's Supper . . .
receive the grace of God in the sacrament . . . the congregation
receives the gift of the body and blood of Jesus Christ, and
receiving that, it receives forgiveness, new life and salvation." [9]
Now all this is perfectly true and valid, and we shall shortly
notice one aspect of it which is also stressed in the liturgical
movement. Nor must we expect here an exhaustive treatment
of the doctrine of the Lord's Supper, for that is not relevant to
Bonhoeffer's intention. It is, however, noticeable that he thinks
of what happens in the Lord's Supper exclusively in terms of
reception. Of course the communicants come to receive. But
not only this. They come to "do" this, the whole action, taking, blessing, breaking, and receiving. One should contrast
what Bonhoeffer says here about preparation for communion
with Bishop John Robinson's sermon preached at the College
Communion on "Preparation for Communion" in *Liturgy
Coming to Life*.[10] Here the act of preparation is related to all
four acts of the liturgy. By contrast, Bonhoeffer is still confined
within the limits of his Lutheran tradition: the Lord's Supper
is exclusively the occasion of receiving.

Nevertheless, there is a dimension even here which is often
lacking in our individualistic pietism. The reception of communion is not seen exclusively in terms of the individual's
communion with his Lord. It entails also communion with
one another: "The fellowship of the Lord's Supper is the
superlative fulfillment of Christian fellowship. As the members
of the congregation are united in body and blood at the table
of the Lord so will they be together in eternity. Here the community has reached its goal." [11] Hence the stress on the confession of sins *within the Christian fellowship*, as the chief act
of preparation for communion, a procedure much healthier
than those questions for self-examination before Holy Communion which found so much vogue in nineteenth-century
Tractarian piety (Have I fasted before communion? Have I

swallowed the water in the glass when cleaning my teeth before communion?).

> The day before the Lord's Supper is administered will find the brethren of a Christian fellowship together and each will beg the forgiveness of the others for the wrongs committed. Nobody who avoids this approach to his brother can rightly go prepared to the table of the Lord. All anger, envy, evil gossip, and unbrotherly conduct must have been settled and finished if the brethren wish to receive the grace of God together in the sacrament.[12]

Here is an authentic scriptural and primitive note. The bishop in the early Christian church, we are told, spent the whole week before the Sunday liturgy endeavoring to reconcile those of his congregation who were at variance one with another. But the purpose of reconciliation was somewhat differently conceived. It was not oriented exclusively toward the reception of communion. It was to do everything humanly possible to make sure that when the faithful exchanged the kiss of peace (which began the eucharistic action and set its keynote) it would be done in sincerity and truth. The whole ensuing action might thus be done by a congregation at unity with itself; not just the receiving of communion.[13] Here is a dimension to the Lord's Supper of which Bonhoeffer is apparently unaware. Or did he, like traditional Lutheranism, reject any (and not only the false medieval) notion of the Eucharistic as the action of the church? We do not know. It is enough to warn us that Bonhoeffer cannot be our exclusive guide for the being of the church in the modern world. There are others from whom we must learn too.

Since the Lord's Supper is brought in so peripherally in *Life Together*, and is apparently not dealt with extensively anywhere else in Bonhoeffer's published writings,[14] it is not surprising that he has nothing to say about its evangelistic or social implications. Yet what is being said in the liturgical movement about these implications is wholly compatible with what Bonhoeffer has to say about both these aspects of Christian responsibility. Bonhoeffer's experiences in prison toward the end of his life had made him highly skeptical of merely verbal communication of the gospel. "The time when men could be told everything by means of words, whether theological or simply pious, is over." Communication of the gospel henceforth must be not so much by words, certainly not the traditional words of theology and religion, but by *being*: "The church is her true self only when she exists for humanity. . . . She must take her part in the social life of the world, not lording it over men, but helping and serving the world." [15] This is what Bonhoeffer called "being there for others." Now there is a real danger that some may take the bit between their teeth and as they read Bonhoeffer come to the conclusion—the old liberal conclusion—that the business of the church is to become a social welfare organization.[16] But "being there for others," as Bonhoeffer means it, is a witness to God's being there for us in Jesus Christ: and this will only be seen where the church's being there for others constantly springs from her own interior life in which God is constantly "there" for her as he was there in Christ, in the Word and sacraments. In other words, it needs liturgy—that point where the church is being truly herself, the community for whom God in Christ is there for her at the center—for the kind of evangelism and social service that Bonhoeffer proposes. Otherwise it will become merely human and humanitarian. Undoubtedly it is this kind of evangelism going hand in hand with a social concern, the witness of the Christian church being the church in the community in which it is set, that must be the evangelism of the future. And here liturgy, as the focal point of the church's life, must be at the heart of it.

Liturgy is pre-eminently the Eucharistic liturgy, in which the totality of Christian worship and the totality of the gospel are exhibited in word and sacrament. It is the church's obedient response to the redemptive act of God in Christ, through which that act is made present. To that she is committed by the very nature of her being, and if she ceases to give that response she ceases to be the church. But in the wisdom of the centuries there has grown up a subsidiary form of devotion, known traditionally as the daily office. In New Testament times, the Christians kept the Jewish hours of prayer. As a devout individual custom this survived till the time of Hippolytus (*Apostolic Tradition* XXXVI, early third century).

In the post-Nicene development of monasticism these private prayers were made into a public service. Hence the monastic daily offices. The custom spread to secular churches: it was made obligatory on all clergy, but never caught on with the secular laity. As *daily* devotions the offices have never in Anglicanism, except in a few places, caught on as daily public services subsidiary (as they were meant to be) to the Sunday Eucharistic liturgy. In European Lutheranism the offices have caught on even less. True, it avoided thereby the unfortunate substitution of the offices for the liturgy which eventually happened in Anglicanism, and preserved at least the *missa catechumenorum* as the central act of Sunday morning worship; a service always had the possibility of being restored to the full Sunday morning liturgy (with Eucharist). Yet from time to time various Lutheran groups have sought to restore the offices, for example, liturgically-minded groups of the esthetic or antiquarian type mentioned earlier in this essay. Bonhoeffer of course would have had little in common with them. And yet, in his pattern of common life at the preacher's seminary, he set up the daily office in all its essentials. The old monastic offices served for the "sanctification of time" (the title of Dix's chapter on the offices in *The Shape of the Liturgy*). Bonhoeffer too aims at the sanctification of time: "The day of the New Testament church begins with the break of day and ends with the dawning light of the next morning. It is the time of fulfillment, the resurrection of the Lord." [17]

So he asks that at the break of day the community come together for common praise, for the common hearing of the word and for common prayer.

Incidentally, here is something particularly worth noting for American Protestants. Any European or Anglican who has had a hand in organizing an ecumenical conference will remember from experience what a barrier to unity is the strange reluctance of American Protestants to meet for worship *before* breakfast! Not so Bonhoeffer: "Common life under the Word begins the common worship at the beginning of the day . . . the deep stillness of morning is first broken by the prayer and song of the fellowship. After the silence of night and early morning hymns and word of God are more easily grasped," and then follows a whole series of Old and New Testament quotations to back up this claim. The forms of worship may vary for different groups: a family with children has different needs from a group of ministers or theologians. But there is a common pattern. It should include the word of Scripture, the hymns of the church, and the prayer of the fellowship. Now, although Bonhoeffer does not make the point, this is exactly the pattern of the daily offices, particularly as they were reformed by Cranmer. It is not just because it is traditional that Bonhoeffer advocates this pattern, but because there is an essential rightness about it: it includes all the elements which make up Christian devotion in its completeness. Note however—and this is also a point which Bonhoeffer has nowhere discussed, though it is implicit in his essay—that this is not the Sunday worship of the church. That, as we have seen, is of a different pattern: it begins with the service of the Word, in which Scripture is used selectively, according to the church year, rather than being read in course, and in which there is preaching, and it culminates in the celebration of the Lord's Supper. The pattern of devotion that Bonhoeffer describes in Chapter II of *Life Together* is not an alternative to the Sunday service: it is the daily devotion of a Christian fellowship, perhaps of a group within the wider congregation, and is ancillary to the Sunday service.

This is exactly the pattern which Cranmer intended, and which has been widely misunderstood in Anglicanism, where Morning Prayer is so often used as an *alternative* to the full Sunday morning service of Word and Eucharist. As Dix has said the office represents the purely *personal* aspect of devotion, and stands quite apart from the corporate worship of the church. This needs to be underlined more than Bonhoeffer has done. The offices are not so much corporate worship as such, but personal devotion done together in a group for mutual edification.

Let us now see what Bonhoeffer has to say about the component parts of this type of devotion. It begins with the Psalms. Bonhoeffer was deeply attached to the Psalms—which is surprising in the German Lutheran Church, where as we have said, the antecommunion (quite rightly) formed the staple of Sunday worship, rather than the office. It is indeed remarkable that Bonhoeffer came to such a deep appreciation of the Psalms, an appreciation which can only have been acquired by a continuous use of them in course. This use in course is exactly what he urges in another little work devoted exclusively to the Psalms, *Das Gebetbuch der Bibel: Eine Einführung in die Psalmen* (1940). We should not, he says, pick and choose, but pray *all* the Psalms, "Otherwise we should dishonor God by presuming to know better than he what we should pray." Bonhoeffer pleads for a recovery of this regular use of the psalter in his own church.

The Psalms are in the Bible, and are therefore the Word of God, but at the same time they are also the prayers of men. This poses a problem, the answer to which is the key to their right use in devotion. A man who uses them will encounter numerous obstacles. As a writer in *Theology* pointed out over twenty years ago,

the worshipper does not necessarily find his own mood
reflected in the appointed psalm. He may be the proud
possessor of an infant son, but the church calls on him to
sing the De Profundis. He may be rejoicing in the agony
of bereavement, and find her rejoicing in the Jubilate.[18]

More than that, there are the imprecatory Psalms. How can a
Christian call forth the vengeance of God upon his enemies as
in Psalm 58 or 109? And then there is the type of psalm which
a sensitive student of the present writer once said irritated him
even more than the imprecatory Psalms, the "As for me"
Psalms, which protest the innocence of the speaker (for example, Psalms 26 and 119).

It is very gratifying to find in this situation Bonhoeffer also
reviving the traditional explanation of the Christian use of the
psalter. For him, too, the Psalms are not prayers of the individual, devout Christian, but the prayers of Christ in his Body
the Church, with which the individual devout worshiper is
called upon to identify himself. Quite rightly, Bonhoeffer
claims that this is what the New Testament and the church
have always declared. The New Testament evidence for this
claim is dealt with more fully in *Das Gebetbuch der Kirche*.
He could very well have added quotations from Augustine and
other Church Fathers, and some of the later evidence from
churches where the psalter has been recited in unbroken and
continuous tradition. This use of the psalter is, as Bonhoeffer
recognizes, something into which one has to grow. It can
hardly be expected of the ordinary Sunday congregation. But
Bonhoeffer was right in advocating the continuous daily use of
the psalter for the kind of group he envisaged in *Life Together*.
He could legitimately expect his students to master the art.

Once it has been mastered, the three difficulties which are
commonly felt with the Psalms are seen in better perspective.
First, the imprecatory Psalms. If we use them as expressions of
our own evil thoughts in a prayer of vengeance, this is of
course unchristian. But "insofar as Christ is in us, the Christ

who took all the vengeance of God upon himself, who met
God's vengeance in our stead, who thus—stricken by the wrath
of God—and in no other way could forgive his enemies, who
himself suffered the wrath of God that his enemies might go
free—we too, as members of this Jesus Christ, can pray these
Psalms, through Jesus Christ, from the heart of Jesus." [19] It
must be confessed that this is a valiant attempt to wrest meaning from these difficult Psalms, but it is hard to see precisely
what it does mean. Who are the enemies against whom, in
Christ, we are to pray for vengeance? It is not possible, without
completely changing the meaning of these Psalms, to use them
as expressions of our sharing in Christ the wrath of God in
order that (presumably) our enemies might be forgiven. Father R. M. Benson has given a more straightforward interpretation of these Psalms, and one which is much easier to use
than Bonhoeffer's:

> The comminatory Psalms are therefore very essential to
> the completeness of the Psalter, for without them the
> mind of Christ, the Redeemer, the Sovereign, and the
> Judge would not be exhibited to us. . . .
> It is not chiefly with reference to others that we repeat
> these Psalms. We have to undergo the final judgment of
> Christ, and we have to consider the necessity of our own
> hearty acceptance of His covenant. There must be in us
> a real love of God, involving the hatred of evil. These
> Psalms remind us of the intensity of the strife wherewith
> the world rages against Christ. It is this strife which we
> have to share.[20]

It is no good beating about the bush. These Psalms pray for
the destruction of enemies, not their forgiveness. But the enemies for whose destruction we pray are not our personal
adversaries. They are the demonic powers of evil, the principal-
ities and powers, the world rulers of this present darkness, the
spiritual hosts of wickedness in the heavenly places. Demythol-
ogize them, interpret them existentially as you will, but do not

eliminate them. And you yourself are involved in them: these Psalms are prayers for the destruction of the evil in your own breast, for the casting of your sins into the depths of the sea. This line of thought is recognized more clearly in *Das Gebet-buch der Bibel:* "The adversaries in question are the enemies of the affairs of God; these Psalms are not concerned with any personal fight. Prayer concerning the vengeance of God has to do with the execution of his righteousness in judgment over sin. . . . It is a judgment under which we stand."

The second difficulty which is cleared up is the problem of the "As for me" Psalms. Can we, asks Bonhoeffer, call our-selves innocent, devout, and righteous? Not as we are in our-selves. But we can insofar as we are in Christ, the sinless one, whose robe of righteousness we have put on ourselves by faith.[21] We might add that insofar as we use them thus, they do not administer to our pride and complacency, but by tes-tifying to us Christ's own sinlessness they awaken in us a greater sense of our own unworthiness, and therefore act as a summons to repentance.

Third, there are the Psalms of suffering. To pray Psalm 22 for instance as though it corresponded to our own experience on a day when we are full of joy (and even on a day of sorrow we are hardly likely to have plumbed those depths) is clearly unrealistic. Again the answer is that we pray them in Christ, and Christ prays them in us. They speak of his sufferings: "all this suffering was real and actual in Jesus Christ, because the Man Jesus Christ suffered sickness, pain, shame, and death." It is because he suffered as a representative Man and because we have died with him in baptism that we have a right to join him in praying these Psalms of the passion: "What happened to us on the Cross of Christ, the death of our old man, and what actually does happen and should happen to us ever since our baptism in the dying of our flesh, *this* is what gives us the right to pray these prayers. Through the Cross of Christ these

Psalms have been bestowed upon his Body on earth as prayers that issue from his heart."

But this use of the Psalms not only overcomes these three difficulties which the ordinary man encounters as he uses them. It also has the positive value of teaching us to pray as a fellowship, as the Body of Christ, rather than as individuals. In this connection Bonhoeffer notes the value of the traditional antiphonal recitation of the psalter. How differently he speaks from the old Puritans who objected to the Anglican "tennis game" and demanded that the Psalms should be read as lessons by the minister! That was a form of sacerdotalism, which paradoxically still prevails in much Free Church worship: the antiphonal way actually gives more effective expression to the priesthood of all believers.

After the recitation of the psalter, the daily devotion proceeds to the reading of Scripture. This is much more than listening to the daily *Losung*, or text of the Moravian brethren which plays such a large part in German Lutheran piety. Bonhoeffer pleads for a longer reading from the Old and New Testaments—at least a chapter of the Old Testament and at least half a chapter of the New Testament every morning and evening. It will be objected that this is more than the individual can assimilate at one go, and that the *Losung* method was better after all. Bonhoeffer answers that we shall not feel this objection if we are really familiar with our Bibles—and continuous reading is precisely the way of becoming familiar with them. Is worship the place for this learning process? Is not this to profane our worship? Bonhoeffer thinks not. It is a daily reminder that this knowledge is something into which we have to grow, something which has to grow upon us. Again, Bonhoeffer pleads for *lectio continua*, for the reading of Scripture as well as the Psalms in continuous course. In this continuous reading of Scripture we are not just reading past history: we participate as God's people today in his dealings with old Israel and in the Christ event. As the scholars of the Roman Catholic liturgical movement would phrase it, we participate in the *mystery* of our redemption. "We are torn out of our own existence and set down in the midst of the holy history of God on earth. There God dealt with us, and there he still deals with us, our needs, and our sins, in judgment and grace . . . we are the reverent listeners and participants in God's action in the sacred storm. . . . And only insofar as we are *there*, is God with us today." [22]

The reading of the Scriptures is followed by the singing of a hymn. Bonhoeffer might have noted that since his scheme provides for two readings from Scripture, one from the Old Testament and one from the New, there should be a hymn after each reading, and it needs to be brought out more clearly than he does, that this hymn is essentially a response to the word in Scripture. It is not quite clear, but it seems that Bonhoeffer is thinking mainly of the canticles. He specifies the Magnificat as one example of the new song. But he makes it clear that he is also thinking of the Reformation Chorales, the hymns of the Bohemian Brethren and those of the ancient church. We should add that the hymn or canticle after the Old Testament lesson should express the sense of Israel's waiting for the fulfillment of the Old Testament, like the Benedictus and the Magnificat, while the hymn after the New Testament lesson should express the church's response to the redemption which has now come in Christ, like the Te Deum or Nunc Dimittis. What Bonhoeffer says about the Word in the hymn would apply with still greater force to the traditional canticles.

Once again, as with the Psalms and the Scripture readings, Bonhoeffer has some wise practical hints on the manner of rendition. The hymn should of course be *sung*. "The fact that we do not speak it but sing it only expresses the fact that our spoken words are inadequate to express what we want to say, that the burden of our song goes beyond all human words." [23] Yet we do not just hum a melody, we sing words: "the music is completely the servant of the Word. It elucidates the Word in its mystery." Bonhoeffer advocates unison singing, a requirement which the traditional plainsong melodies to the canticles would satisfy. Only unison singing can express the unity of the Body. Here he has some rude though amusing things to say about people who show off by singing in parts. We all know them. Yet, we should add, there is some value in really good polyphonal singing. That too can express the unity of the Body as Paul understands it in I Corinthians 12:14-27.

Finally, as in the traditional offices, comes the common prayer. "We have heard God's Word, and we have been permitted to join in the hymn of the Church; but now we are to pray to God as a fellowship, and this prayer must be our word, our prayer for this day, for our work, for our fellowship, for the particular needs and sins that oppress us in common, for the persons committed to our care."[24]

With this stress on the immediate concrete situation, it is not surprising that Bonhoeffer pleads for free prayer: "Good and profitable as our restraints may be in order to keep our prayer pure and Biblical, they must nevertheless not stifle necessarily free prayer itself, for Jesus Christ attached a great promise to it." Here Bonhoeffer departs from the tradition, which knows only fixed collects at this point. Each method has its dangers. We all know that the fixed collects can degenerate into a dead, mechanical routine. Bonhoeffer is of course aware of this. He writes:

> The use of formal prayer can, under certain circumstances, be a help even for a small family group. But often a ritual becomes only an evasion of real prayer. The wealth of churchly forms and thought may easily lead us away from our own prayer; the prayers then become helpful and profound, but not genuine. Helpful as the church's tradition of prayer is for learning to pray, it nevertheless cannot take the place of prayer I owe to God this day.[25]

But some of us also know that the free prayer of the individual can tyrannize over the congregation—we are forced to pray *his* prayers to identify ourselves with his sentiments (and they are often very sentimental): there can be just as great an air of unreality about free prayer as about the fixed prayer. How can we avoid the pitfalls of either method, yet preserve the here-and-now concrete relevance of free prayer with the objective, corporate (and, it must be said, biblical) character of the traditional collect? Here, we would plead, the primitive church has something to teach us. Following earlier synagogue practice, it proceeded thus:

> First, a subject was announced, and the congregation was bidden to pray. All prayed silently on their knees for a while; then on the signal being given, they rose from their knees, and the officiant summed up the petitions of all in a brief collect. They knelt to pray as individuals, but the corporate prayer of the church is a priestly act, to be done in the priestly posture for prayer, standing. Therefore all, not the celebrant only, rose for the concluding collect.[26]

Admittedly this type of prayer was used in the synaxis, the Sunday gathering of the church which preceded the Eucharist, but it could also be tried out at the daily offices. It seems to combine the virtues while avoiding the pitfalls of both free and fixed prayer, as neither Bonhoeffer's suggestion nor the traditional method does.

Quite rightly, Bonhoeffer treats first the corporate devotional life of the Christian family, and only then does he pass on to individual devotion; for corporate prayer, as the Lord's Prayer itself teaches (Our Father . . . give *us*, forgive *us*, lead *us* not, deliver *us*) is the norm of Christian prayer, and private prayer is an extension of the corporate. The need for private devotion is usually, though somewhat superficially, justified on the ground that it is only such personal devotion that can preserve our participation in corporate devotion from becoming mechanical. Bonhoeffer probes deeper, and defines their relation in terms of community and solitude, speech and silence.[27] Community unbalanced by solitude means only escape from loneliness into the collective: "only as we are within the fellowship can we be alone, and only he that is alone can live in the fellowship." Speech without silence becomes chatter. Silence is not dumbness, but silence under the Word. (This whole section is to be commended to retreat conductors). The purposes of silence are threefold: Scripture meditation, prayer, and intercession.

First, meditation. *Here* is the place for the *Losung*, the brief selected text. Here we "expose ourselves to the specific word until it addresses us personally." For the clergy Bonhoeffer has the wise advice that this must not degenerate into sermon preparation! And there is more wise advice, which is found in all the classic treatments of meditation in Counter-Reformation spirituality (and it is none the worse for that). Meditation need not issue in vocal prayer: "Unphrased thought and prayer, which issues only from our hearing, may often be more beneficial." In meditation it is not necessary to discover new ideas. Even an already familiar word can penetrate and dwell within us, working in us all day long often without our being conscious of it. We must not necessarily expect extraordinary experiences in meditation. Bonhoeffer is fully aware of the "dryness" of which all the classical devotional writers speak. And he recommends the same way of dealing with them: perseverance. Through dryness we learn to seek God, not consolations; God sometimes withdraws the consolations in order that we may seek him. Bonhoeffer might add that the person who passes through dryness generally thinks that he is the only soul whom God has dealt with thus, and might point out that even the greatest saints have known these periods.

Out of meditation spring prayer and intercession. Prayer which follows on meditation is prayer delivered from our own emptiness. This prayer differs from the prayer of the fellowship, in that it concerns our own personal situations, particular tasks, decisions, sins, and temptations. Here (though this might come more suitably in the earlier section on meditation) Bonhoeffer deals with the problem of distraction. We are not to be discouraged and give up meditation when our thoughts wander, nor should we try to "snatch back our thoughts convulsively, but quite calmly to incorporate into our prayer the people and the events to which our thoughts keep straying and thus in all patience return to the starting point of the meditation." This is what all the great masters of the spiritual life tell us.

From petitionary prayer we pass to intercession: not the common intercessions of the fellowship, but the special intercessions for those to whom we as individuals owe a special responsibility. In a close-knit fellowship, such as Bonhoeffer contemplates, this especially means those brethren with whom we are in tension or estrangement. Our intercessions should be as definite and concrete as possible. Intercession, Bonhoeffer hints, and we should like to bring it out clearly, means participation in the redemptive purpose of God for those for whom we pray; it is real work. And, as he himself emphasizes, it is especially the task of the pastor for the members of his congregation. Do we think of our pastoral task as exhausted if (in one tradition) we prepare our Sunday sermon? Or, in another tradition, if we say our daily Mass? Bonhoeffer stresses the *pastoral* over the priestly and the prophetic conception of the ministry. We must be regular and systematic about intercession, setting apart a regular time for it.

Finally, the test of meditation, Bonhoeffer insists—and it is a characteristic point which is not often made in the traditional teaching—is the effect it has on us when we are alone in an unchristian environment. Here is no cloistered piety (whether of the medieval monastery, of the country rectory, or of the hothouse seminary) but a pattern of life for Christians in the modern world. The only question we would ask is, How far is such a life possible time-wise for the busy Christian today? How far does the classical pattern, upon which Bonhoeffer draws so heavily, presume the leisure of the convent, of an Oxford college, or of a spacious nineteenth-century parsonage with its numerous domestic servants? A modern clergyman of the "pastoral director" type [28] could perhaps achieve it by getting his priorities straight. But what of the busy layman in the modern world? In fairness to Bonhoeffer it must be remembered that he was writing for a seminary. But one of the urgent needs of the church is for a *viable ascetic*, and here Bonhoeffer does not give us much help. He might have done just this had he been spared Flossenbürg and related *Life Together* to the insights of *Prisoner for God*.

In the last chapter of *Life Together* Bonhoeffer discusses the place of confession and absolution in the life of the fellowship. The primary justification he gives for specific confession is characteristic: "The pious fellowship permits no one to be a sinner. So everybody must conceal his sin from himself and from the fellowship. We dare not be sinners. Many Christians are unthinkably horrified when a real sinner is suddenly discovered among the righteous. So we remain in our sin, living in lies and hypocrisy." [29] A good description of our suburban captivity! So Bonhoeffer advocates the private confession of sin. Not however, as in the tradition, exclusively to the priest. The authority of John 20:23 [30] is given for all Christ's followers. So it is to the brother that the Christian should go for confession. This was certainly the New Testament practice (James 5:16). In some of our traditions (and this is true even in Bonhoeffer's German Lutheranism) this practice is normally confined to the minister. This is not only justifiable on grounds of expediency: it is also because he alone can speak with the authority of the whole congregation behind him as its commissioned representative.

Bonhoeffer is aware of this dimension: "I meet the whole

congregation in the one brother to whom I confess my sins and who forgives my sins. In this matter no one acts in his own name nor by his own authority, but by the commission of Jesus Christ. The commission is given to the whole congregation and the individual is called merely to exercise it for the congregation." We would contend that normally it is the minister who has this authority. But in any case it must be a brother who is under the Cross who hears the confession. It is, Bonhoeffer insists, only those who submit themselves to this discipline who should administer it to others.

Like all ordinances within the church, and like all devout practices, specific confession has its advantages and pitfalls. Bonhoeffer deals with both. First, it enables a man to "break through to community." Instead of bottling up his sin to himself, he brings it out and coughs it up. Only so can it be dealt with. Instead of leaving him to fight his battle alone, the community takes it upon itself. The sin concealed separated him from the fellowship: now that it is confessed he is restored. Bonhoeffer does not think that it is necessary for the restoration of the penitent to fellowship that he should make public confession of his sins before the congregation. Maybe in the type of community that Bonhoeffer had immediately in mind in *Life Together* such public discipline was never necessary!

The second advantage of specific confession before a brother is that it brings home to the sinner the shame of his sin: "Confession in the presence of a brother is the profoundest kind of humiliation. It hurts, it cuts a man down, it is a dreadful blow to pride." [31] We are reminded of the remarks on cheap grace at the beginning of *The Cost of Discipleship*.

The third advantage of such confession is that we hear the word of absolution coming to us from outside. We are not tempted to "grant ourselves absolution," another expression of cheap grace.

One can recognize the force of this argument. But historically the system of private absolution grew up in the sixth century from an amalgam between two older practices, the public discipline and absolution mentioned above, and a less formal practice in which less serious sins were confessed to a spiritual director without absolution.[32] The difficulty with this developed system (which Bonhoeffer uncritically takes from the traditional Western practice) is that it reduces private absolution to a doublet of one aspect of the reception of communion (Matthew 26:28), an aspect that is emphasized in all liturgies, particularly in Lutheranism. Consequently there is much to be said in favor of recent pleas for a reversion to pre-sixth century practice, involving (a) the restoration of public discipline with special absolution in the case of scandalous sin and (b) the restoration of "spiritual direction." The spiritual director would hear the confession of sins, but absolution would be deferred until it is received in communion. Such a spiritual director may, but need not be, an ordained minister. This arrangement, incidentally, would obviate our misgivings about the authority of a lay person to pronounce absolution in the name of the whole congregation.

The present Archbishop of Canterbury has said that the next goal of the ecumenical movement must be the deepening of the spiritual life in the divided portions of the Body of Christ in order that we may all be worthier of the unity for which we hope and pray. Bonhoeffer, being dead, yet speaketh. He has not all the answers, but he has many important things to say on liturgy and devotion to the ecumenical movement as it enters the post-New Delhi phase.

Notes for Essay 7

1 Dietrich Bonhoeffer, *Prisoner for God: Letters and Papers from Prison*, Reginald H. Fuller, tr. (New York: The Macmillan Company, 1953), p. 77.

2 Since the reform of the Holy Week Services in 1955 this is no longer the case.

3 Reprinted with the permission of the publisher from *Prisoner for God: Letters and Papers from Prison*, p. 105, by Dietrich Bonhoeffer, tr. by Reginald Fuller. Copyright 1953 by The Macmillan Company. All other excerpts from *Prisoner for God* in this essay are used by permission.

4 *Ibid.*, p. 148.

5 Beginning with the scholarly researches of the European Benedictines the ideas of this movement were first mediated to the English-speaking world by A. G. Hebert's *Liturgy and Society* (London: 1935). Then came Dom Gregory Dix's monumental *Shape of the Liturgy* (London: Dacre Press—A. & C. Black Ltd., 1945), which, though sometimes to be used with caution, is a scholarly simplification of the basic insights of the modern scholarship behind the liturgical movement.

6 John A. T. Robinson, *Liturgy Coming to Life* (London: A. R. Mowbray, 1960), p. 37.

7 *Prisoner for God (op. cit.)*, p. 41.

8 If a seminary or other enclosed community desires to break the bread more frequently, it must be understood to bear the same relation as the "House Church" celebration bears to the Parish Communion. See John A. T. Robinson, "The House Church and the Parish Church" in *On Being the Church in the World* (London: Student Christian Movement Press, 1960).

9 Dietrich Bonhoeffer, *Life Together*, John Doberstein, tr. (New York: Harper & Brothers, 1954), pp. 121f.

10 John A. T. Robinson (London: A. R. Mowbray, 1960), pp. 79-82.

11 *Ibid.*

12 *Ibid.*

13 On the kiss of peace in the early church. See G. Dix *(op. cit.)*, pp, 105ff.

14 But see the sacramental references in the essay by J. Pelikan in this book. It is tantalizing that the "Outline for a Book" in *Prisoner for God*, pp. 178-181, has just this reference to worship: 2(d) Cultus (Details to follow later, in particular on cultus and religion), p. 179. Bonhoeffer was speaking here just in

the context where we would have wished to hear him: of the liturgical being of the Church in a world come of age. Cf. the question (not answered) on p. 123, "What is the place of worship and prayer in an entire absence of religion?"

15 *Prisoner for God* (op. cit.), pp. 122, 180.

16 For Bonhoeffer's criticism of the American social gospel see Hans J. Hildebrand, "Dietrich Bonhoeffer in America" in *Religion and Life*, XXX No. 4 (Autumn, 1961).

17 *Life Together* (op. cit.), pp. 40ff.

18 Kenneth N. Ross, "The Sunday Offices and the War," *Theology* XVI, No. 241 (July, 1940), p. 72.

19 Dietrich Bonhoeffer, *Life Together*, John Doberstein, tr. (New York: Harper & Brothers, 1954), p. 47. Used by permission of the publisher. All other excerpts from the book in this essay are by permission of Harper & Brothers.

20 *The War Song of the Prince of Peace* (London, 1901), Vol. I, 306 and 276. In public domain.

21 *Life Together*, p. 48.

22 *Ibid.*, pp. 53f.

23 *Ibid.*, p. 59.

24 *Ibid.*, pp. 62f.

25 *Ibid.*, p. 65.

26 G. Dix, *Shape of the Liturgy* (London: G. Allenson, Ltd., 1945), p. 42.

27 *Life Together*, pp. 76ff.

28 See H. Richard Niebuhr, "The Merging New Conception of the Ministry," in *The Purpose of the Church and Its Ministry* (New York: Harper & Brothers, 1956).

29 *Life Together* (op. cit.), pp. 110ff.

30 The primary reference here is doubtless to baptismal forgiveness, though insofar as absolution of postbaptismal sin is an extension of this primary forgiveness, the text may perhaps be legitimately extended to cover this also. Bonhoeffer's exegesis, though traditional, is incautious.

31 *Life Together* (op. cit.), p. 114.

32 See J. G. Davies (op. cit.), p. 196. His résumé of the development is based on K. E. Kirk, *The Vision of God* (London: 1937); G. Rauschen, *Eucharistie und Bussakrament in den ersten sechs Jahrhunderten der Kirche* (Freiburg: 1908); B. Poschmann, *Die abendländische Kirchenbuss im frühen Mittelalter* (Munich: 1928); R. C. Mortimer, *The Origins of Private Penance* (Oxford: 1939).

8

The Christian in the World Responding
to the Answer in Jesus Christ

Perhaps Bonhoeffer's whole career would today appear to have been
less fragmentary, more systematic in its theological contribution had
he from the first concentrated on theological ethics. For a long time
he seemed to know that this was the orientation and goal of his
thought, his vocational destiny. For a long time he had been called to
"live" Christian ethics in a complex world; only just before the end
—when death prevented him from completing his work—did he embark on the task of writing in this field. Yet all the earlier work: the
sociology of the Church; the methodology of theology; the biblical concern for discipleship; the disciplines of devotion—all these pointed to
the Ethics.

The task of relating Ethics to the nonreligious interpretation of the
Christian faith is also least difficult, for it overlaps in part the period
of the last letters and in fact in its later stages explicitly informs Bonhoeffer's discussion of a world come of age, in which Jesus Christ moves
in the concrete experience of the Christian. His tendencies to reject
the attitudes, stances, presuppositions, metaphysics associated with
pious or religious Christianity were fulfilled and realized in the Ethics.
His distinction between "ultimate" and "penultimate" matters liberated him for the concern for the world—as parallel concerns had freed
Augustine and Luther in whose lineage he stood in this matter.

If his whole theological task was concerned with the concreteness
of revelation in Jesus Christ, now he was given a partial chance to depict its appearance in the world of men. George Forell of the School
of Religion in the State University of Iowa has written extensively in
the field of ecclesiology and ethics. Among his books are The Protestant Faith, Faith Active in Love, and Ethics of Decision. Though
Forell regards Bonhoeffer, quite naturally, more positively than do some

of the writers who explore Bonhoeffer's work in disciplines where he was less at home, the author of this essay also brings a detachment to the analysis. Despite the parallel sources and concerns of their ethical thought, Forell has evidenced little conscious influence of Bonhoeffer in his own writings. The congeniality of this author with this subject suggests that in the future he may!

Realized Faith, the Ethics of Dietrich Bonhoeffer

By George W. Forell

"RARELY perhaps has any generation shown so little interest as ours does in any kind of theoretical or systematic ethics." [1] When Bonhoeffer wrote these opening words of his *Ethics* they expressed his reaction to the superabundance of concrete ethical problems which had paralyzed the theologians. From the beginning of the disclosure of the hollowness of Western civilization in 1914 until 1945 when the "Third Reich" collapsed, the rush of events had given no one the leisure to analyze the situation. Bonhoeffer saw his time as an age of villains and saints. "Shakespeare's characters walk in our midst," he said, "but the villain and the saint have nothing to do with systematic ethical studies. They emerge from primeval depth and by their appearance they tear open the infernal or the divine abyss from which they come and enable us to see for a moment into mysteries of which we had never dreamed." [2] In the final blast of the eruption of the infernal from primeval depth Bonhoeffer himself was murdered.

We ask now, What were the types of theoretical or systematic ethics which Bonhoeffer had in mind when he made this critical observation and which in his judgment elicited so little interest in his time? If one limits the discussion to Christian ethics, there were in the main four types of ethical systems offered to Bonhoeffer's generation. They are essentially the same which are still offered to us today, though further elaborated during the breathing spell after Bonhoeffer's death, when for a moment the abyss seemed to close, affording some time for reflection and an opportunity for some major and many minor voices to make themselves heard in an effort to explain the nature and task of the Christian in the world.[3]

But what are these types of theoretical or systematic ethics which Bonhoeffer considered and apparently found wanting? There is first of all the massive Thomistic moral theology of Roman Catholicism as represented by the many revised and yet substantially ever the same editions of Joseph Mausbach's *Katholische Moraltheologie*. The ninth edition under the supervision of Professor Gustav Ermecke appeared in 1959.[4]

Here ethics is rooted in ontology. The activity of the creature is the unfolding of its being and participation in the creative activity of God. As far as man is concerned, the source of his ethical responsibility is his freedom. "Moral action is the personal, reasonable, free action of Man (material object) measured by the moral standard (formal object).[5]

The moral standard is the divine law which is based upon the order of being and value. Man has access to the good life by way of reason and conscience. Conscience is essentially the judgment of practical reason concerning the morality of one's own actions. Thus the ethical life is accessible to all men. Though all values are rooted in God there has to be no explicit understanding of this connection in order to perceive the reality and the obligatory character of ethics. "The possibility of such [natural-moral good action] derives from everything that has been said as being basic for morality especially from the fact of conscience and free will." [6]

Here Christian ethics is an improvement through grace of the good moral life essentially possible for all men. Ethics is feasible because of the ontological connection between God and man. Because it is true of all men that God is the creator and man the creature, all men are created for the good life. The task of moral theology is to help reason to be truly reasonable and to sharpen the conscience. For those who are Christian there is available, in addition, the supernatural grace of the sacramental life. But it is through an analysis of being, with its origin and destiny in God, that we find our way to the good life.

Strangely enough, much of the so-called Neo-Protestant ethics operates in a similar fashion. It proceeds from a general human ethics, a philosophical ethics, to a specific Christian ethics. The latter is an improvement, a purification, a fulfillment of the former. This is illustrated by the words of a typical representative of this "Neo-Protestantism," the Marburg theologian, Georg Wünsch. He wrote, "As everything has the origin of its being in God and no creature can disown the creator, there is no opposition in kind between natural, i.e. this worldly, immanent morality as directed by naturalistic and human criteria, and, on the other hand, Christian morality as determined by the being of God." [7] Bonhoeffer knew this type of ethical approach and clearly rejected it. He opposed any kind of "abstract ethic." "Christ did not love a theory of good, but He loved the real man. He was not, like a philosopher, interested in the 'universally valid,' but rather in that which is of help to the real and concrete human being." [8] "What can and must be said is not what is good once and for all, but the way in which Christ takes form among us here and now. The attempt to define that which is good once and for all has, in the nature of the case, always ended in failure." [9] Bonhoeffer gave as a reason for this failure that "either the proposition was asserted in such general and formal terms that it retained no significance as regards its contents, or else one tried to include in it and elaborate the whole immense range of conceivable contents, and thus to say in advance what would be good in every single conceivable case; this led to a casuistic system so unmanageable that it could satisfy the demands neither of general validity nor of concreteness." [10] With the first observation he repudiated the formalism and vagueness of all Neo-Protestant ethics and with the latter he dismissed casuistry with its unavoidable tendency to substitute a complicated system of avoidance of evil deeds for a simple and direct conformity with the Incarnate which is "achieved only when the form of Jesus Christ itself works us in such a manner that it molds our form in its own likeness. (Galatians, 4:19)" [11]

A second system of ethics which Bonhoeffer rejected he himself frequently called "pseudo-Lutheran." It is the ethics dominated by a kind of spatial thinking which divides reality as a whole into two parts, and "the concern of ethics is with the proper relation of these two parts to each other." [12] Though spatial thinking in its scholastic form subjects the realm of nature to the realm of grace, and in its spiritualistic-enthusiastic form divides the congregation of the elect from the hostile world, in the "pseudo-Lutheran" scheme "the autonomy of the orders of this world is proclaimed in opposition to the law of Christ." [13] Christian ethics has nothing to say to man in his social and cultural involvements. In these areas man must act in obedience to their autonomous laws. It is only in the realm of the spirit and of the soul that the Christian faith has a significant contribution to make. Although Ernst Troeltsch falsely attributed this ethics of the "double morality" to Luther,[14] it was in fact an approach associated with some German Lutherans since the nineteenth century. F. Naumann, for example, wrote, "Every one of us is a servant in many realms and in those realms must obey an iron compulsion, a power of logic, which is contained in the situation itself. But wherever we are free from such compulsion and logic, wherever we have the feeling that our path is not determined there is the part of our life where we want to be first of all servants of Christ." [15] Mentioning Troeltsch and Naumann by name, Bonhoeffer opposed an ethic which by its spatial thinking reduced the Christian ethic to a "purely religious" power indifferent and unconcerned with regard to worldly institutions and conditions.[16] It was especially in the formulation which Otto Dilschneider [17] had given it that Bonhoeffer rejected this ethical approach. "Evangelical ethics," Dilschneider had said, "is concerned with man's personality and with this personality alone. All the other things of this world remain untouched by this Evangelical ethos. The things of the world do not enter ethically into the zone of ethical imperatives." [18] Bonhoeffer repudiated this position categorically because he considered the isolation of the person from the world of things idealistic and not Christian. A doctrine which states that the arena of things is in principle the arena of *adiaphora* he considered antinomian. And he believed that the terms "person" and "thing" were untheological terms, inappropriate to this kind of discourse, which did not help to clarify the task of ethics but rather tended to confuse it. Calling this entire approach "pseudo-Lutheran" he said:

> So long as Christ and the world are conceived spatially as areas adjacent to each other and repelling each other man will be left in the following dilemma: he abandons reality as a whole, and places himself in one or the other of the two spaces. He seeks Christ without the world, or he seeks the world without Christ. In either case he is deceiving himself. Or else he tries to stand in both spaces at once and thereby becomes the man of eternal conflict, the kind of man who emerged in the period after the Reformation and who has repeatedly set himself up as representing the only form of Christian existence which is in accord with reality.[19]

As an alternative to a view of mutually repellent contiguous spaces, Bonhoeffer insisted that that which is Christian can be "found only in that which is of the world, the 'supernatural' only in the natural, the holy only in the profane, and revelational only in the rational." [20] This does not mean, however, that the natural is identical with the supernatural or the revelational with the rational. "But between the two there is in each case a unity which derives solely from the reality of Christ, that is to say solely from faith in this ultimate reality." [21]

A third option among the systematic interpretations of Christian ethics which was very familiar to Bonhoeffer was the ethics of Karl Barth. There are some observers who have placed Bonhoeffer in close proximity to Barth and have suggested that Bonhoeffer's ethics is actually a variation of Barthian Christocracy.[22] Barth's ethics is characterized by the attempt to derive Christian ethics from Christology. He says, "The goodness of human action consists in the goodness with which God acts toward man. But God deals with man through His Word. . . . Therefore man does good in so far as he hears the Word of God and acts as a hearer of this Word." [23] And a little later he continues, "Man does good in so far as his action is Christian. A Christian is one who knows that God has accepted him in Jesus Christ, that a decision has been made concerning him in Jesus Christ as the eternal Word of God, and that he has been called into covenant with Him by Jesus Christ as the Word of God spoken in time." [24] The concrete application of this Barthian ethics has probably received its most famous formulation in his booklet *The Christian Community and the Civil Community*, first published in 1946 and now included in *Community, State and Church*.[25] Here we see a most lucid application of Barth's Christocratic ethics to the problem of the relationship of Church and State. Barth states that political organization can be neither a repetition of the Church nor an anticipation of the kingdom of God.[26] He suggests that the State must be regarded "as an allegory [*Gleichnis*], as a correspondence and an analogue to the Kingdom of God which the Church preaches and believes in." [27] He claims that the State is ignorant of the mystery of its own center (it is the outer circle, within which the Church, with the mystery of its faith and gospel is the inner circle) yet through the distinctions, judgments, and choices which the Church makes in the political sphere it illuminates "the State's connection with the order of divine salvation and grace" and discourages all the attempts to hide this connection.[28] In Barthian ethics the state is to be molded into an allegory of the kingdom of God. The criterion for ethical action in the state (or in any other ethical decision) [29] is its contribution to the clarification of the Lordship of Christ over the whole. Even the Church's political activity is therefore

> a profession of its Christian faith. By its political activity it calls the State from neutrality, ignorance, and paganism into co-responsibility before God, thereby remaining faithful to its own particular mission. It sets in motion the historical process whose aim and content are the moulding of the State into the likeness of the Kingdom of God and hence the fulfillment of the State's own righteous purposes.[30]

Barth is quite ready to illustrate what criteria for the State he can discover in the Gospel:

1. From the story of the Good Samaritan he concludes that the Church when active in politics will be interested in human beings and not in abstract causes.[31]

2. From the fact of divine justification Barth concludes that the Church will support that State "which is based on commonly acknowledged law, from submission to which no one is exempt, and which also provides equal protection for all." [32]

3. Since Christ came to seek and to save the lost, the Church will insist on the State's special responsibility for the weaker members of society. "The Church must stand for social justice in the political sphere. And in choosing between the various socialistic possibilities (social-liberalism? co-operativism? syndicalism? free trade? moderate or radical

Marxism?) it will always choose the movement from which it can expect the greatest measure of social justice (leaving all other considerations on one side)." [33]

4. Since the Church is the fellowship of those who are freely called, it affirms as the basic right which every citizen must be guaranteed by the State, the freedom to carry out his decisions in the politically lawful sphere, according to his own insight and choice, and therefore independently, and the freedom to live in certain spheres (the family, education, art, science, religion, culture), safeguarded but not regulated by law.[34]

5. The Church is the Body of Christ and it understands the relationship between the head and the members in organic terms, and this means in politics a transcendence of both individualism and collectivism.

6. Because it is the fellowship of those who live in one faith under one Lord on the basis of one Baptism "the Church must and will stand for the equality of the freedom and responsibility of all adult citizens, in spite of its sober insight into the variety of human needs, abilities and tasks." This means also the granting of political rights to women.[35]

7. Since the Church knows the variety of gifts and tasks of the one Holy Spirit it will advocate checks and balances, the separation of the legislative, executive, and judicial powers.[36]

8. Since Christ is the Light of the World the Church must oppose all secret policies and secret diplomacy.[37]

9. Since the Church is established and nourished by the free Word of God it must advocate freedom of speech in the political life.[38]

10. Since the members of Christ's Church do not rule but serve, the legitimate use of power in the political community must always be a form of service.[39]

11. "Since the Church is ecumenical (catholic) by virtue of its very origin it resists all abstract local, regional, and national interests in the political sphere." [40]

12. "The Church knows God's anger and judgment, but it also knows that his anger lasts but for a moment, whereas His mercy is for eternity." For this reason it will support violent political solutions only when they are for the moment the ultimate and only possibility available. "The perfections of the Father in heaven, who does not cease to be the heavenly Judge, demands the earthly perfection of a peace policy which really does extend to the limits of the humanly possible." [41]

We have given Barth's method of political ethics in such detail because only then does it become quite obvious that Bonhoeffer's ethics, in spite of many superficially similar formulations, has little in common with this peculiar effort to derive the political credo of social-democratic liberalism from the structure of the kingdom of God. Using Barth's method one could easily give Christian endorsement to "free-enterprise economic conservatism" or "absolute monarchy." Church history bears eloquent witness to the fact that with the help of the methodology of analogical interpretation anything can be demonstrated, depending on the political idiosyncrasies of the particular theologian. For Bonhoeffer the ethical task of the State cannot be discovered by an exegetical analysis of the biblical assertions concerning the kingdom of God and their analogical application to the State, the "moulding of the State into the likeness of the Kingdom of God." [42] Bonhoeffer says, "Good is not the correspondence between a criterion which is placed at our disposal by nature or grace and whatever entity I may designate as reality. Good is reality itself, reality seen and recognized in God." [43] Bonhoeffer operates with the distinction between what he calls the "ultimate" and the "penultimate" (*Die letzten und die vorletzten Dinge*). God's justification by grace and faith alone is this ultimate word.[44] But this word reaches a person who lives his life in the "penultimate." The "things before the last" have, indeed, no value of their own, but they are related to the ultimate. To remain in the realm of the penultimate rather than to find ultimate solutions may be the way to "point all the more genuinely to the ultimate, which God will speak in His own time (though indeed even then through a human mouth)." [45] To illustrate this point he says:

> Let us ask why it is that precisely in thoroughly grave situations, for instance when I am with someone who has suffered a bereavement, I often decide to adopt a "penultimate" attitude, particularly when I am dealing with Christians, remaining silent as a sign that I share in the bereaved man's helplessness in the face of such a grievous event, and not speaking the biblical words of comfort which are, in fact, known to me and available to me. Why am I often unable to open my mouth, when I ought to give expression to the ultimate? And why, instead, do I decide on an expression of thoroughly penultimate human solidarity? Is it from mistrust of the power of the ultimate word? Is it from fear of men? Or is there some good positive reason for such an attitude, namely, that my knowledge of the word, my having it at my finger tips, in other words my being, so to speak, spiritually master of the situation, bears only the appearance of the ultimate, but is in reality something entirely penultimate? [46]

It would appear that in Bonhoeffer's terms Barth's Christocratic ethics operates too hastily with the ultimate in order to make it supply the criteria for ethical action. Barth himself, though expressing real appreciation of Bonhoeffer's *Ethics*, is aware of basic differences and has criticized Bonhoeffer's concept of the divine *mandates* (see below) as somewhat arbitrary and reflecting "north German patriarchialism." [47]

A fourth ethical approach known to Bonhoeffer and also a present option is the ethics of existentialism in all its various forms. Here we must restrict our discussion to the forms of religious existentialism which base ethics upon the "courage to accept acceptance" (Tillich) in the face of the various anxieties which always threaten man. Confronted by ethical decision the Christian's faith proclaims

> a voice out of the depth of our situation, elevating our concrete problems into an ultimate perspective. In doing so, it probably has devaluated some factors determining our decision and has stressed others. Or it has left the balance of possibilities unchanged, but has given us the courage to make a decision with all the risks of a decision, including error, failure, guilt.[48]

Christian ethics is here the call to authentic selfhood. The Lord from whom you desire a word, "wants you to decide for yourselves." [49] Similarly Schubert Ogden says, "Man is a genuinely free and responsible being, and therefore his salvation is something that, *coram deo*, he himself has to decide by his understanding of his existence." [50]

As far as Christian ethics is concerned this means that it is built around the courageous overcoming of the anxieties of fate and death, of emptiness and meaninglessness of guilt and condemnation. The Christian analysis of life moves into close proximity to those of the depth analysts and the modern artist, who are so very much concerned with man's dependence, helplessness, and enslavement by social, psychological, and hereditary powers over which he has no control. A distinction between pathological and existential anxiety is frequently made,[51] but ethics deals here with the helplessness in the borderline situations of human existence. Anxiety is seen as the clue to the understanding of man and the overcoming of anxiety through courage as the ethical action *par excellence*. The result is that for this type of ethics Kierkegaard and his existentialist followers are as important as Aristotle is for Thomistic ethics. Just as a Thomist has to convert the prospective believer first to the dubious metaphysics of Aristotle before he can confront him with the Gospel of Christ, the Christian existentialist is committed to the philosophy of

Kierkegaard, Nietzsche, or Heidegger, and must convert man to their analysis of the human situation before he can proclaim to him the Gospel of the new life in Christ.

Did Bonhoeffer know this ethical approach, and did he have anything to say in this regard? It seems that he knew it very well and attacked it as a form of illegitimate "methodism" not only in his *Ethics* but in some of his last writings, in his letters from prison.[52] In the *Ethics* Bonhoeffer speaks of justification as the last word. In making his distinction between the ultimate and the penultimate he sees no logical or automatic progress from the penultimate to the ultimate.

> The event of the justification of a sinner is something final. . . . God's compassion on a sinner must and can be heard only as God's final word; for otherwise it is not heard at all. . . . This word implies the complete breaking off of everything that precedes it, of everything that is before the last; it is therefore never the natural or necessary end of the way which has been pursued so far, but it is rather the total condemnation and invalidation of this way.[53]

For Bonhoeffer there is no metaphysical or existential analysis of the human situation which prepares the way for the final word of justification. All these analyses are judged by God's final word. They are inappropriate in what he called the "world come of age." In a letter of June 1, 1944, he wrote:

> Efforts are made to prove to a world thus come of age that it cannot live without the tutelage of "God." Even though there has been surrender on all secular problems, there still remain the so-called ultimate questions—death, guilt—on which only "God" can furnish an answer, and which are the reason why God and the Church and the pastor are needed. But what if one day they no longer exist as such, if they too can be answered without "God"? [54]

Then he speaks of what he calls

> the secularized offshoots of Christian theology, the existentialist philosophers and the psychotherapists who demonstrate to secure, contented, happy mankind that it is really unhappy and desperate, and merely unwilling to realize that it is in severe straits it knows nothing at all about, from which only they can rescue it. Wherever there is health, strength, security, simplicity, they spy luscious fruit to gnaw at or to lay their pernicious eggs in. They make it their object first of all to drive men to inward despair, and then it is all theirs. That is secularized methodism.[55]

Bonhoeffer rejected this approach because he felt it reached only those whom he called a small number of "intellectuals and degenerates." Furthermore he considered the approach pointless, ignoble and unchristian: "When Jesus blessed sinners," he said, "they were real sinners, but Jesus did not make every man a sinner first. He called them out of their sin not into their sin." [56] It may be debatable whether Bonhoeffer did justice to the existentialist concern in these somewhat unguarded letters, which were, after all, not written for publication, but it is apparent that he knew the approach and found it wanting.

Thomistic-ontological ethics, pseudo-Lutheran spatial ethics, Barthian Christocracy, and Christian existentialism—all these approaches to the Christian life seemed inadequate to Bonhoeffer. He felt that the customary ways of dealing with ethics led nowhere:

> An ethic cannot be a book in which there is set out how everything in the world actually ought to be but unfortunately is not, and an ethicist ("*Ethiker*") cannot be a man who always knows better than others what is to be done and how it is to be done. An ethic cannot be a work of reference for moral action which is guaranteed to be un-

exceptionable and the ethicist cannot be the competent critic and judge of every human activity.[57]

This detached view seemed to him utterly unwarranted by the clue to Christian ethics, the deed of God in Christ. From prison Bonhoeffer wrote:

> Man is challenged to participate in the sufferings of God at the hands of a godless world. He must therefore plunge himself into the life of a godless world without attempting to gloss over its ungodliness with a veneer of religion or trying to transfigure it. He must live a "worldly" life and so participate in the suffering of God. He may live a worldly life as one emancipated from all false religions and obligations. To be a Christian does not mean to be religious in a particular way, to cultivate some particular form of asceticism (as a sinner, a penitent or a saint), but to be a man. It is not some religious act which makes a Christian what he is, but participation in the suffering of God in the life of the world.[58]

Here, then, is the key to Bonhoeffer's ethics. It is realized faith and thus participation in the suffering of God. Ethics has its source in the encounter with Christ, the Incarnate, the Crucified, the Risen One. Because Christ is the *Incarnate* it is man's right and duty that he should be man. Bonhoeffer rejected the quest for the superman, the endeavor to outgrow the man within the man, the pursuit of the heroic, the cult of the demigod—because of the Incarnation. "The real man is at liberty," he says, "to be his Creator's creature. To be conformed with the Incarnate is to have the right to be the man one really is." [59]

Because Christ is the *Crucified*, conformation to Him means being a man sentenced by God. Man dies every day the death of a sinner. "He cannot raise himself up above any other man or set himself up as a model, for he knows himself to be the greatest of all sinners." All suffering that comes to him man bears in the knowledge that it serves to enable him to die with his own will, to let God be true. Only "in surrendering himself to God's judgment upon him and against him is he himself just in the eyes of God." [60]

Because Christ is the Risen One conformation to Him means to be a new man before God. "In the midst of death he is in life. In the midst of sin he is righteous. In the midst of the old he is new." All this is a secret which remains hidden to the world. This new life is "hidden with Christ in God" (Colossians 3:3). And in a world in which Christ's glory is hidden to the eyes of the world even he who is conformed with the Risen One has only an occasional glimpse of the glory that is to come.

> The new man lives in the world like any other man. Often there is little to distinguish him from the rest. Nor does he attach importance to distinguishing himself, but only to distinguishing Christ for the sake of the brethren. Transfigured though he is in the form of the Risen One, here he bears only the sign of the cross and the judgment. [61]

Bonhoeffer's ethics is an ethics of the cross rather than an ethics of glory. Man does not become God, but because God became man, man can become man. This takes place in the Church. "The Church is nothing but a section of humanity in which Christ has really taken form. The Church is the man in Christ, incarnate, sentenced and awakened to new life." [62]

But since it is an ethics of the "cross" and not of "glory," the Church is not set up, so to speak, as a model for the world. "What is of ultimate importance is now no longer that I should become good, or that the condition of the world should be made better by my action, but that the reality of God should show itself everywhere to be the ultimate reality." [63] "But God as the ultimate reality is no other than

He who shows forth, manifests, and reveals Himself, that is to say, God in Jesus Christ." [64] This means that "the problem of Christian ethics is the *realization* [*Wirklichwerden*] among God's creatures of the revelational reality [*Offenbarungswirklichkeit*] of God in Christ, just as the problem of dogmatics is the *truth* of the revelational reality of God in Christ." [65] And in a sweeping distinction between Christian ethics and all other ethics Bonhoeffer asserts:

> The place which in all other ethics is occupied by the antithesis of "should be" and "is," idea and accomplishment, motive and performance, is occupied in Christian ethics by the relation of reality and realization [*Wirklichkeit und Wirklichwerden*], past and present, history and event (faith), or, to replace the equivocal concept with unambiguous name, the relation of Jesus Christ and the Holy Spirit. The question of good becomes the question of participation in the divine reality which is revealed in Christ.[66]

On the basis of this central significance of reality and realization for Christian ethics, what does Bonhoeffer have to say about the multitude of decisions that confront man? Are they all to be handled in the light of this participation in the divine reality? He proceeds with this distinction between the ultimate and the penultimate (see above) and refuses to rush into penultimate questions with ultimate answers; for when this is done nothing is really said, and the ultimate answer is not really ultimate if applied in such an irresponsible fashion. Bonhoeffer objects to a "pan-ethical" approach which assumes that every moment of life involves a conscious decision between good and evil. Calling the ethical phenomenon a "peripheral event" (*Grenzereignis*) he objects to the assumption "that a man must continually be doing something decisive, fulfilling some higher purpose and discharging some ultimate duty." [67] Such an approach fails to understand that in historical human existence, "everything has its time (Ecclesiastes 3), eating, drinking and sleeping as well as deliberate resolve and action, rest as well as work, purposelessness as well as the fulfillment of purpose, inclination as well as duty, play as well as earnest endeavor, joy as well as renunciation." The "pan-ethical" approach misjudges this pattern of creaturely existence and leads either to the "most mendacious hypocrisy or else to madness. It turns the moralist into a dangerous tormentor, tyrant and clown, a figure of tragicomedy." [68] Bonhoeffer, therefore, advocates the avoidance of the overburdening of life by the ethical, since otherwise the result is an "abnormal fanaticization" and a "total moralization of life."

What Bonhoeffer suggests instead is an analysis of the natural, the form of life preserved by God after the Fall. Here he deals with natural life, the *suum cuique*, the right to bodily life, the problem of suicide, reproduction, and nascent life, freedom of bodily life, and the natural rights of the life of the mind. This section remained unfinished but reveals Bonhoeffer's concern with specific ethical decisions. It is in the context of this analysis that he offers his view of the "structure of responsible life." [69] Responsible life is a life of deputyship (*Stellvertretung*). An ethics which deals with man as if he were an isolated individual is a fiction. But this life of deputyship is open to two abuses, the absolutizing of one's own ego or of the other man. If this happens, "there is a denial of the origin, the essence and the goal of responsible life in Jesus Christ, and responsibility itself is set up as a self-made abstract idol." [70]

Responsible life is life in correspondence with reality (*Wirklichkeitsgemässheit*). Here Bonhoeffer insists that responsibility does not mean the illusion that one has some ethical principle at one's disposal which one can "put into effect fanatically, overcoming all the resistance which is offered to it by reality." [71] "For the responsible man the given situation is not simply the material on which he is to impress his idea or his programme by force, but this situation is itself drawn into the action and shares in giving form to the deed." [72] This does not mean some *Realpolitik* which identifies the opportune and successful with correspondence to reality.

> The true meaning of correspondence with reality lies neither in servility towards the factual nor yet in a principle of opposition to the factual, a principle of revolt against the factual in the name of some higher reality. . . . In action which is genuinely in accordance with reality there is an indissoluble link between the acknowledgment and the contradiction of the factual. The reason for this is that reality is first and last not lifeless; but is the real man, the incarnate God.[73]

Action which is in accordance with Christ is in accordance with reality because it allows the world to be the world. This does not mean a view of the autonomy of various areas of life but rather a vision of the simplicity of life—as reconciled by Christ.

> The world remains the world because it is the world which is loved, condemned and reconciled in Christ. No man has the mission to overleap the world and to make it into the kingdom of God. Nor, on the other hand, does this give support to that pious indolence which abandons the wicked world to its fate and seeks to rescue its own virtue. Man is appointed to the concrete and therefore limited responsibility which knows the world as being created, loved, condemned and reconciled by God and which acts within the world in accordance with this knowledge.[74]

Bonhoeffer denied that it is the Christian's task to "turn the world upside down" but he insisted rather that he had to do what is necessary at the given place and with due consideration of reality. Such correspondence with reality demanded pertinent action (*Sachgemässheit*) as well as the readiness to accept guilt and freedom. But this was done in the place of responsibility, where God has called man, in his vocation or calling.

In a final chapter which was left unfinished the place where God calls man was further elaborated. It is where God orders life through concrete commandment. Bonhoeffer suggested four mandates, the Church, marriage and the family, culture, and government. He preferred this term of mandate to the more common terms of estate (*Stand*) or office (*Amt*) because the latter "suggest human prerogatives and privileges and no longer convey their original meaning of dignity and humility." [75] But the injection of the concept of mandate reveals Bonhoeffer's sensitivity to the divinely structured character of reality. Even though he was not allowed to develop these ideas fully the fragments available indicate that also in his ethics, "the cross of atonement is the setting free for life before God in the midst of the godless world; it is the setting free for life in genuine worldliness." [76]

If we now ask what Bonhoeffer's *Ethics* can contribute to the theological discussion in the second half of the twentieth century we must observe first of all that Bonhoeffer's criticism of the ethical systems of his time remains relevant. Thomistic-ontological ethics, pseudo-Lutheran spatial ethics, Barthian Christocracy, and Christian existentialism have eloquent advocates today. Bonhoeffer's critique remains valuable. To make conversion to Heidegger's philosophy the condition for the Christian faith and life is no more cogent than to depend on Aristotelian metaphysics, and the particular political idiosyncrasies which Barth manages to derive from the biblical witness by means of his analogical method seem no more convincing than the diagrammatic spatial thinking of what Bonhoeffer called the "pseudo-Lutherans." Bonhoeffer's criticism is important and helpful. But did he do more? Did he suggest a positive direction which Christian ethics ought to follow in order to fulfill its mission in our world?

Following Gerhard Ebeling,[77] one could suggest that Bonhoeffer raises the central problem of Christian ethics, namely the proper distinction of Law and Gospel, in a new manner uniquely appropriate to our situation in the twentieth century. In the *Ethics* he wrote, "Just as in Christ the reality of God entered into the reality of the world, so, too, is that which is Christian to be found only in that which is of the world, the 'supernatural' only in the natural, the holy only in the profane, and the revelational only in the rational." [78] But he continued by saying that what is Christian is not identical with the supernatural or the revelational with the rational. Between the two, however, there is in each case a unity which derives solely from the reality of Christ, that is to say solely from the faith in this ultimate reality." [79] Bonhoeffer sees the unity in the way in which the secular and the Christian elements prevent one another from assuming any kind of static independence in their relation to each other. They are polemically related and thus bear witness to their common reality, their unity in the reality in Christ. It is here that Bonhoeffer sees himself taking a stance very similar to Luther's:

> Luther was protesting against a Christianity which was striving for independence and detaching itself from the reality in Christ. He protested with the help of the secular and in the name of a better Christianity. *So, too, to-day,* when Christianity is employed as a polemical weapon against the secular, this must be done in the name of a better secularity and above all it must not lead back to a static predominance of the spiritual sphere as an end in itself.[80]

Only as a polemical unity can Luther's doctrine of the two kingdoms be accepted, and Bonhoeffer was convinced that it was so intended. Thus the proclamation of the Law must not be allowed to deteriorate into legalism, and the proclamation of the Gospel must not deteriorate into purely religious speech separated from the worldly existence of man. "This false antithesis of moralizing and religious themes must be replaced by the true distinction and connection between the law and the gospel." [81]

How does all this fit in with Bonhoeffer's final concern with "nonreligious interpretation" as evidenced in his letters from prison? One could say religious interpretation is legalistic or moralistic interpretation as it confronts us in our age. Nonreligious interpretation attempts the proper distinction between Law and Gospel, which is ultimately always God's accomplishment rather than man's. Luther said once in a remark at table reported by Johannes Schlaginhaufen:

> There isn't a man on earth who knows how to distinguish between Law and Gospel. We assume that we know how to do it when we hear it preached but we miss greatly. Only the Holy Spirit knows this. The man Christ was also unable to make this distinction that time on the mountain so that an angel had to come and comfort him. Though He was the Doctor from heaven, yet He had to be strengthened by the angel. I often supposed that I could do it since I have written so much about it, but when it comes to making this distinction accurately I must admit that I miss it very, very far. Thus God must alone be and abide the most holy master. [82]

Bonhoeffer follows suit by saying, "Ultimately it is not the preacher but God alone who distinguishes between the law and the gospel." [83]

To modern man it is the problem of religion which has taken the place of the problem of the Law as illustrated in Paul's letters by the controversy about circumcision. Paul tried to disentangle Christianity from the legalism which was suffocating the faith of his people, the Jews. Luther was engaged in essentially the same effort in his attack against salvation by works, which threatened to undo the Church in his time. The distinction between Law and Gospel seemed to him the only device which could possibly reveal the hopelessness of all work righteousness and all theology of glory. Bonhoeffer saw the Christian faith disappearing in the quicksand of religiosity, from the so-called "positive Christianity" of the official political platform of the National Socialist party to the repristination of the "old-time religion" by the pietists. He wrote, "The Pauline question whether circumcision is a condition of justification is today, I consider, the question whether religion is a condition of salvation. Freedom from circumcision is at the same time freedom from religion." [84] For Bonhoeffer, religion is a space on the border of human existence reserved for God. He claims that religious people speak of God when human perception is (often just from laziness) at an end, or human resources fail. He objected to the God who fills the gaps. This he did in all his theological work, and this is the concern of his *Ethics* as an ethics of the cross. "This is the decisive difference between Christianity and all religions. Man's religiosity makes him look in his distress to the power of God in the world; he uses God as a *Deus ex machina*. The Bible, however, directs him to the powerlessness and suffering of God; only a suffering God can help." [85]

But an ethics of the cross is an ethics which distinguishes Law and Gospel.

> It is only when one knows the ineffability of the name of God that one can utter the name of Jesus Christ. It is only when one loves life and the earth so much that without them everything would be gone, that one can believe in the resurrection and a new world. It is only when one submits to the law that one can speak of grace, and only when one sees the anger and wrath of God hanging like grim realities over the head of His enemies that something of forgiveness and love for the enemy can touch our heart. He who tries to think and feel too speedily and directly in New Testament terms is in my judgment not a Christian. . . . One cannot and must not speak the ulti-

mate word before one has spoken the penultimate. We live in the penultimate and believe in the ultimate.[86]

Bonhoeffer was willing and able to make distinctions between the penultimate and the ultimate, Law and Gospel, the world and God; and yet he knew that there are not two realities but only one, and that is the reality of God, which has become manifest in Christ in the reality of the world. As one who knew the difference between Law and Gospel and the unity of the one God who gives reality to both, Bonhoeffer restated what Luther and Paul had proclaimed before him. But by seeing God's claim in the context of a world come of age in which men have to live as if there were no God he addressed the task in a fresh way opening up the possibility of stating the ethics of the cross for our age with precision and passion.

Notes for Essay 8

1 Reprinted with the permission of the publisher from *Ethics*, p. 3, by Dietrich Bonhoeffer, edited by Eberhard Bethge, tr. by Neville Horton Smith. Copyright 1955 by The Macmillan Company. All other excerpts from *Ethics* in this essay are used by permission.

2 *Ibid.*, p. 3.

3 Since Bonhoeffer a number of major "systematic ethics" have appeared: e.g., Karl Barth, *Die Kirchliche Dogmatik* III, 4 (1951); W. Elert, *Das Christliche Ethos* (1949); A. De Quervain, *Ethik* (1942 ff.); H. Thielicke, *Theologische Ethik* (1951ff.). It is not without significance that Thielicke opens his many-volumed effort with the words, "Unless all signs deceive, the emphasis in theological research is now shifting to the problem of ethics" (Vol. I, v.).

4 Joseph Mausbach, *Katholische Moraltheologie*, ninth improved edition by Gustave Ermecke (Münster: Aschendorfsche Verlagsbuchhandlung, 1959).

5 Mausbach-Ermecke (*op. cit.*), I, 65.

6 *Ibid.*, I, 281.

7 Georg Wünsch, *Theologische Ethik* (1925), pp. 122f., as quoted in Karl Barth, *Church Dogmatics*, Vol. II, Sec. 2, p. 534f. (Edinburgh: T. & T. Clark, 1957).

8 Bonhoeffer, *Ethics* (*op. cit.*), p. 22.

9 *Ibid.*, p. 23.

10 *Ibid.*

11 *Ibid.*, p. 18.

12 *Ibid.*, p. 62.

13 *Ibid.*, p. 62.

14 Ernst Troeltsch, *The Social Teachings of the Christian Churches*, 2 vols. (London, 1931).

15 F. Naumann, *Briefe Über Religion* (Berlin, 1916), as quoted in Georg Wünsch: *Evangelische Ethik des Politischen* (Tübingen, 1936), p. 359.

16 Bonhoeffer, *Ethics* (*op. cit.*), p. 287.

17 Otto Dilschneider, *Die evangelische Tat* (Gütersloh, 1940), p. 87.

18 As quoted in Bonhoeffer, *Ethics* (*op. cit.*), p. 286.

19 *Ethics* (*op. cit.*), p. 63 (translation modified).

20 *Ibid.*, p. 65.

21 *Ibid.*

22 Jürgen Moltmann, "Herschaft Christi und soziale Wirklichkeit nach Dietrich Bonhoeffer," Theologische Existenz Heute, N.F. 71 (Munich: Chr. Kaiser Verlag, 1959).

23 Karl Barth, Church Dogmatics, Vol. II, Part 2 (Edinburgh: T. & T. Clark, 1957), p. 546.

24 Ibid., p. 547.

25 Karl Barth, Community, State and Church, Will Herberg, ed. (New York: Doubleday & Co., Inc.—Anchor Books, 1960).

26 Ibid., p. 168.

27 Ibid., p. 169.

28 Ibid., p. 170.

29 Cf. Karl Barth, Die kirkliche Dogmatik, Vol. III, Part 4 (Zurich: Evangelischer Verlag, 1951).

30 From Community, Church and State by Karl Barth. Copyright © 1960 by The National Student Christian Federation. Reprinted by permission of Doubleday & Co., Inc.

31 Ibid., pp. 171f.

32 Ibid., p. 172.

33 Ibid., p. 173.

34 Ibid., p. 174.

35 Ibid., p. 175.

36 Ibid.

37 Ibid., p. 176.

38 Ibid.

39 Ibid., p. 177.

40 Ibid., p. 178.

41 Ibid.

42 Ibid., p. 171.

43 Bonhoeffer, Ethics (op. cit.), p. 59.

44 Ibid., p. 84.

45 Ibid., p. 85.

46 Ibid., pp. 84f.

47 Karl Barth, Die kirchliche Dogmatik, Vol. III, Part 4, pp. 21ff.

48 Paul Tillich, The New Being (New York: Charles Scribner's Sons, 1955), pp. 118f. Used by permission.

49 Ibid., p. 119.

50 Schubert Ogden, Christ Without Myth (New York: Harper & Brothers, 1961), p. 136.

51 Cf. Paul Tillich, Courage to Be (New Haven: Yale University Press, 1952, p. 77.

52 Dietrich Bonhoeffer, Prisoner for God: Letters and Papers from Prison, Eberhard Bethge, ed. (New York: The Macmillan Company, 1954).

53 Bonhoeffer, Ethics (op. cit.), p. 84.

54 Reprinted with the permission of the publisher from Prisoner for God: Letters and Papers from Prison, p. 146, by Dietrich Bonhoeffer, tr. by Reginald Fuller. Copyright 1953 by The Macmillan Company. All other excerpts from Prisoner for God in this essay are used by permission.

55 Ibid., p. 146.

56 Ibid., p. 156.

57 Ethics (op. cit.), p. 236.

58 *Prisoner for God (op. cit.)*, p. 168.
59 *Ethics (op. cit.)*, p. 19.
60 *Ibid.*, p. 19.
61 *Ibid.*, p. 20.
62 *Ibid.*, p. 21.
63 *Ibid.*, p. 55.
64 *Ibid.*, p. 56.
65 *Ibid.*, p. 57.
66 *Ibid.*
67 *Ibid.*, p. 232.
68 *Ibid.*, p. 233.
69 *Ibid.*, pp. 194ff.
70 *Ibid.*, p. 196.
71 *Ibid.*, p. 197.
72 *Ibid.*
73 *Ibid.*, p. 198.
74 *Ibid.*, p. 202.
75 *Ibid.*, p. 254.
76 *Ibid.*, p. 263.
77 Gerhard Ebeling, "*Die Nicht-religiöse Interpretation biblischer Begriffe*" in *Die Mündige Welt*, Vol. II (Munich: Chr. Kaiser Verlag, 1956), pp. 12-73.
78 Bonhoeffer, *Ethics (op. cit.)*, p. 65.
79 *Ibid.*
80 *Ibid.*
81 *Ibid.*, p. 283.
82 *Luther's Works*, Weimarer Ausgabe, Tischreden, Vol. 2, p. 4, No. 1234.
83 Bonhoeffer, *Ethics (op. cit.)*, p. 280.
84 Bonhoeffer, *Prisoner for God (op. cit.)*, p. 123.
85 *Ibid.*, p. 164.
86 *Ibid.*, p. 79 (translation modified).